the Everlasting God

Broughton Knox

We're delighted to make this wonderful book available to you. I pray that it will be profoundly helpful to you in your relationship with God and in your pastoral ministry. It certainly has been in my life and ministry. In fact, I've lost count of the number of times I've read this book with other Christians.

Just as *The Trellis and the Vine* introduced you to Matthias Media's theology and philosophy of Christian ministry, we hope *The Everlasting God* will also show you the doctrine of God that is central to our theological foundations.

Sincerely

Marty Sweeney

Ministry Director
Matthias Media (USA)
Toll free: 1 866 407 4530

The Everlasting God

Matthias Media
(St Matthias Press Ltd ACN 067 558 365)
PO Box 225
Kingsford NSW 2032
Australia
Telephone: (02) 9233 4627; international: +61 2 9233 4627
Email: info@matthiasmedia.com.au
Internet: www.matthiasmedia.com.au

Matthias Media (USA)
Telephone: 330 953 1702; international: +1 330 953 1702
Email: sales@matthiasmedia.com
Internet: www.matthiasmedia.com

A note on Bible versions
In the course of his lectures and writings, Dr Knox characteristically quoted from either the King James Version or the Revised Version, and sometimes in a combination of both. We have retained this feature.

ISBN 978 1 921441 49 3

Cover design and typesetting by Matthias Media.

Contents

preface

The Everlasting God

When I first read *The Everlasting God* in the mid-1980s, it blew my mind. It made my previous conception of who God was seem like a crude children's jigsaw with half a dozen pieces. Here, by contrast, was a 1000-piece puzzle of a complexity and beauty that I hadn't thought possible. And yet the overall effect was not to confuse or confound, but to see the whole picture with a new clarity and sense of awe.

It was (and remains) the best-known literary work of Broughton Knox, who at that time was something of a living legend among Sydney evangelicals. He had shaped a generation of students at Moore College during his 26 years as Principal (1959-85), and wielded an extraordinary influence over the character and direction of Reformed evangelical Christianity in Sydney and beyond. Former Archbishop of Sydney Sir Marcus Loane wrote of him: "It is not too much to say that no other contemporary Australian churchman has had a more original mind or has shown a more penetrating insight into questions of pure theology, and that insight was derived from his understanding of the supreme revelation of truth in the Bible".

Broughton Knox died in 1994, and *The Everlasting God* fell out of print for a time. It was republished in 2000 in volume 1 of Matthias Media's edition of *D. Broughton Knox Selected Works*, and is now available in this new stand-alone edition.

It is not a difficult book to read, but not a quick book to

read either. The language is straightforward, but the ideas are probing, challenging, mind-stretching, profound. It is a book to savour and ponder, with a Bible open. It is also worth noting that Dr Knox did not consider the structure or organization of *The Everlasting God* to be definitive or comprehensive. On being criticized, for example, for not including more on the doctrine of the Spirit, he responded: "I must emphasize that this book is a reprint of five lectures given to a lay audience. The five subjects chosen are subjects of importance, but I could not choose every subject of importance on the doctrine of God. But they were subjects which I believed needed emphasis in the context of my hearers. The Spirit is God, and what is said of God is said of the Spirit."

My hope and prayer is that this new edition of *The Everlasting God* will find a new generation of readers, eager to deepen their knowledge of God, and ready to have their minds blown.

Tony Payne
Matthias Media
May 2009

chapter 1

The living and true God

The doctrine of God is of the utmost importance, for it controls the whole of life. As a person thinks about God, that is to say, as he thinks about ultimate reality, so his standards of behaviour, values and relations with other people are determined.

Everyone has a doctrine of God, even if it is only the negative doctrine that God does not exist. On such a view, the objectives and values of life and relationships with other people will be very different from what they are when ultimate reality is conceived as a personal God who will judge the world by his standards of right conduct, which are written in the human conscience. On the other hand, if a person's doctrine of God has the Christian dimension of self-sacrificing love, then behaviour and attitudes will again be different from what they would be without a belief in the existence of God. Everyone has a doctrine of God, that is, of ultimate reality, which will influence every aspect of life—the emotions, the decisions of the will, the hopes of the future and day-to-day behaviour. If the thinker is consistent, so that his actions correspond with his thoughts, then his doctrine of God will control his behaviour completely. But most of us are inconsistent, and this does not add to our happiness or enhance our effectiveness.

Since this doctrine is so influential, and a true doctrine consistently held and practised is a source of great benefit, it is a matter of great importance to investigate what may be known of the character and nature of God.

Deity is a concept congenial to the human mind. The existence of divine being is not an abstruse or difficult concept, like, for example, that of the infinitesimal calculus, which has to be struggled with before it can be apprehended; for even the simplest and youngest mind finds the notion of deity easy to accept and to understand. The idea of deity may be said to be innate, not in the sense that a child is born with the idea fully formed in his mind, but in the sense that the concept is readily understood and accepted by the child as soon as he is told about it. Strictly speaking, it is responsiveness to the concept of deity which is innate, though in actual fact there has been no child born into the world who has not early in his life learned from his elders of the concept of deity. For religion and belief in the divine are co-extensive with humanity. As far back into history as we can push our knowledge of the human race, religion is found, and among the nations and tribes that make up humanity at the present day, religion is a universal activity. So every child, early in his life, comes to hear of the concept of deity, and when he hears he understands it, and he has little problem in accepting it, if he learns it from one with whom he is in sympathy.

The ingredients that make up this universally held concept include personality and everlastingness, as well as knowledge, power and relatedness. The deities, as humanity conceives of them, are eternal, superhuman beings who influence our lives and who in turn may be influenced by a right approach to them. Belief in the existence of such a being or beings is found throughout humanity. There is no race known to history, or to archaeology, or to anthropology, who did not or who does not believe in deity. The concept is filled out in different ways, and apart from Christianity, Judaism and Islam, deity is always conceived of as a plurality of divine beings. Only in the sophisticated society of the ancient world or of modern times has the reality of deity been denied.

Although it obviously would be to the advantage of self-centred humanity that deity should not exist, the notion of deity is so natural to the human mind that the acceptance of its non-existence can only be maintained by constant propaganda, and even this fails and the concept returns in one form or other. It would be strange indeed if this universal and tenacious concept of deity had no correspondence with reality. The alternative to the reality of deity is that people have made up the belief because their nature needs it. But this explanation contains within it a contradiction. For if people's nature is solely the creation of their environment, as the atheist affirms, how does it come about that the real environment has created in humans a need which can only be satisfied by something which does not exist—a need so real and basic that no human race has existed without its fulfilment in religious belief? The environment has not done this for any other form of life. How are we to believe then that it should do so simply for human life? It is self-contradictory to believe that ultimate reality, in this case for the atheist, material reality, has shaped humanity so that man is only truly man, only truly human, only truly related in a human way in societies, and only prospers, if he believes and devotes himself in worship to a nonentity, to something which is not there at all. If such were the case with regard to humanity, *homo sapiens* would be a sardonic misnomer.

Personal deity self-revelational

Although sophisticated thought is able to arrive at the concept of impersonal deity, and ultimately at the concept of the non-existence of deity, the universal view of deity, as received among the nations of the world from the time that history began, is that deity is personal. Now if this is true, it follows that men can have no knowledge of deity apart from deity's own volition. The gods have always been conceived of as persons, yet persons cannot be known unless they reveal themselves. To reveal themselves or not to do so remains within the will of persons.

Similarly, if the universally held view of humanity is true, if deity not only exists but is personal, the possibility follows that deity may reveal itself to humans. This possibility is inherent in personality. We ourselves, being persons, may take the initiative and reveal ourselves to whom we will; so, too, with personal deity, it may reveal itself to whom it will. But, of course, such events are unpredictable, just as our own decision to speak to this one, but not to that one, is unpredictable. The matter rests entirely within ourselves. But once deity has acted to reveal itself, then the event passes into history. From that moment on, it is an historical event which cannot be eliminated with the passage of time. It is written in the ongoing pages of history. Now in the history that is written in the Scriptures it is affirmed that deity has addressed itself to humans in this way. For example, while Abraham was living with his relatives, idol-worshippers in Mesopotamia beyond the river Euphrates, God Almighty spoke to him, and commanded him to leave his home in Ur and his kinsmen, and to go out into a land which God would show him, and Abraham believed God and obeyed.

In this way, through this word and response, Abraham, who up until then had been ignorant of God, began to know God. It is plain from the Old Testament narrative that God spoke with Abraham on many subsequent occasions. Abraham's personal relationship to God was so full that he was called the "friend of God".[1] Indeed this was God's own designation of Abraham: "Abraham my friend".[2] Friendship arises through personal conversation, personal association, one speaking to the other, the other responding, and vice versa. God took the initiative and spoke to Abraham, Abraham responded, and the friendship began which deepened over the years as Abraham came to know God more and more.

Another example from the history of the Old Testament of God's taking the initiative to make himself known was the incident of the burning bush in the desert of Sinai. Here God spoke to Moses, told Moses his name and something of his character, gave him directions how he should act and commissioned him to lead his people out of Egypt. Subsequent revelation of God to Moses was so complete and full that God himself said of Moses that he spoke to him face to face like a friend speaks to a friend.[3] A third example is at Mount Sinai where God addressed the children of Israel directly, giving them the Ten Commandments.[4]

Persons are self-authenticating

We could multiply such illustrations, but it is sufficient to say that, when a person addresses another person, such

1 Jas 2:23
2 Isa 41:8
3 Exod 33:11; Num 12:8; Deut 34:10
4 Exodus 19-20

action carries with it its own authentication. We know this from our own experience. So, too, when God addresses anyone, the person knows that he is being addressed. All necessity for proof of the existence of God falls away when you meet God. What is true on a human level when we meet with one another is all the more true when God, the Creator on whom we depend, wills to meet and speak with us his creatures and to establish personal relationships with us. Those to whom God speaks will have a firm and clear conviction of God's existence and of the fact that he is addressing them. God's words are self-authenticating to the hearts and minds of those whom he addresses. It could not be otherwise. When God spoke to Abraham, there could not be a moment's doubt in his mind that God was speaking to him, any more than there could be in Paul's mind any doubt that the Lord Jesus was addressing him on the Damascus road. So, too, with Moses and with all those to whom God speaks.

God's word authenticates itself, and must do so, because it is a personal word addressed to a person and heard by that person, for that is the purpose of God's speaking, and his purposes do not fail. Personal words addressed to us by someone else, when received as personal words, carry within themselves their self-authenticating character; that is to say, when we hear someone addressing us, we know the reality of the existence of that other person, and if we listen to him we become, by the act of listening, personally related to him. So, too, when God addresses people, God's existence is known by those who hear, with a conviction which all theories can never attain. The universal view of humanity drawn from their contemplation of creation, namely that deity exists, is proved to be true at the moment that God addresses us, as he addressed Abraham, as he addressed Moses and as he addresses all his children.

When the superhuman Person whom we know as God addresses any one of us, in that approach by God to us, in that word which he speaks to us, and which we receive because it is addressed to us by our Creator, we know God to be the true and living God. We know that he exists, we know that he has addressed us, we know that he is the living God, the true God, for only the living and true can speak. The gods of the philosophers never come to life. We cannot relate ourselves to them because they do not address us. They are dead. They do not exist. The same is true of the gods of the idolaters, only more conspicuously so. As the psalmist says, "They have mouths but they do not speak".[5] They do not address us; they are non-gods. But the God who addresses us is known in that action not only to be, but to be the living God and the true God, and we know that we are in his presence.

God is known in his Word

Humanity's universal belief in deity, that is, in a superhuman person of everlasting character, of power and in a relationship with us, is confirmed as true in the only way that it can be confirmed—namely, by the deity approaching us and establishing a relationship with us through personal intercourse—that is to say, through his word, for words are the medium of personal relationship. God has spoken and in that address to us we know him—we know him to be

5 Ps 135:16

existent, we know him to be living and we know him to be the only true God, because his Word carries conviction and he affirms that he alone is God. We know this to be true because, knowing him, we know his character—that he is true.

God has not confined himself to speaking to Abraham and to Moses, but he has continued to speak to those whom he has chosen to address, and he has made known abundantly what his character is, through this ongoing relationship of person to person. In the same way as we learn the character of a friend as years go on and as our fellowship with our friend deepens, so, too, God has spoken to his people through the centuries in different ways. The most characteristic way by which God's Word came in Old Testament times was through prophets; that is to say, through the men and women in whom God's Spirit dwelt and whose words were controlled by the Spirit of God so that they were God's words though also remaining the words of the prophet. The prophet prefaced what he had to say with the introductory phrase "Thus saith the Lord" and then went on directly to speak in the first person singular in God's name. So the prophet was, as it were, God's mouthpiece, and those who heard the prophet heard God, and in hearing God's words learned of God's character. Now the Spirit of God was both giving the words through the prophet and confirming the words in the hearts of those to whom they were addressed.

The phenomenon of prophecy was not an occasional occurrence among the people of Israel but was characteristic of their relationship to God. God was present in the words of his prophets and the people were related to their divine Lord through his Word. As the Hebrew text so quaintly puts it, God rose up early and sent his prophets.[6] There was a succession of prophets right through Old Testament times who through their messages made clear the character of God and his will for men, and in this way gave to the hearers the opportunity of response through faith and obedience and so brought them into a personal relationship with the God who gave the Word.

The movement of the true and living God in revelation of himself to humanity was not confined to the prophets, but reached its apex in the incarnation of the Son of God himself. In Jesus of Nazareth God was present with us. Jesus was Emmanuel and his words were the words not of a prophet, but of the divine Creator himself. No longer does the divine message need the preface of "Thus saith the Lord", but Jesus speaks directly with the divine 'I': "I say unto you".[7] Christ's words were the words of God, and were received as such by those who believed him. In the words of Jesus and in the example of his life, God spoke to us, revealing his character and his will for us, and enlarged the possibilities of our relationship with him.

The revelation of God in Jesus was completed through the apostles and New Testament prophets. Jesus himself foretold that the Spirit of God, whom the Father would send at the Son's request on his ascension, would lead the apostles into the fullness of truth about those things which he himself could not yet teach them because of their immaturity. And so it came about. The Spirit of prophecy was conspicuously present among New Testament Christians.

6 As reflected in the KJV rendering of Jeremiah 7:13.
7 Matt 5:21-22, 27-28

The inscripturated living Word

But there is a further point to add. God not only spoke directly to Abraham and to Moses, and to the children of Israel at Mt Sinai. He not only spoke through the prophets and once again directly in the Lord Jesus Christ, but he has spoken to us also, through the written Word of Scripture. We meet with him in his Word, which he addresses to us. The lifeless, the dead, the fictional gods of the nations do not speak. We may speak about them, theorize about them, mythologize about them. But the true and living God speaks, not only in the past but in the present also, for he has inscripturated his Word in the Bible. The Bible does not become out of date. It is the Word of God to the present-day reader, for what was spoken, for example, to Moses, was spoken by God not only to Moses, but also to us. Thus Jesus, quoting from Exodus, asked the Sadducees, "Have you not read that which was spoken to you by God?"[8] The writing may be ancient, but today's reader meets God in that Word, for God speaks to him in it and this was the divine intention from the time the Word was first spoken centuries before.

The Scripture is the true Word of God, as true a word as the word that Moses or Abraham heard or as Isaiah spoke in the name of the Lord, indeed as true a word of God as Jesus spoke (and expressed in his life) in Galilee. This is a great comfort. The words that Jesus spoke are no longer available for us to listen to with our outward ears, as the disciples did, nor can our eyes observe his character. Undoubtedly Jesus is pre-eminently the Word of God. Yet we can no longer observe his actions, and his words have

8 Matt 22:31

ceased to echo in the Galilean hills. The words that Moses heard have similarly perished. But what we do have is the imperishable written Word, and our Lord and the apostles unite in affirming that this written Word is as prophetic a word as the word that was spoken for example by Isaiah, as true a divine word as that which was spoken by Jesus or his apostles, or uttered by God directly from heaven at Sinai or to Moses in the desert. As Paul put it, the written Word of Scripture is God-breathed, just as our words are breathed by us.[9] He called the Scriptures the oracles of God, that is, divine statements, spoken by God himself.[10] This is in fact the uniform testimony of all the New Testament writers. In this they were following the teaching of Jesus, who taught that what was said in the Scripture was spoken by God to us and that it could not be falsified.[11] It is essential for Christians not to deviate by a hairsbreadth from what Jesus taught about God, for he is the divine Son of God, and if he is wrong in what he believed and taught about God and God's relation to his creation, his words can carry no intrinsic authority in any other sphere of his teaching. Now with regard to Scripture, Jesus taught that this feature of creation is related to God in a way which makes the words in every respect God's words. It follows that the Scripture then, as the Word of God, is infallible, and without error in all that it affirms. The character of its divine Author assures the reader of its truth and reliability. The reader knows *a priori* that it is true, that is, that it is infallible.

9 2 Tim 3:16
10 Rom 3:2
11 Matt 19:4-5, 22:31; John 10:35

The Bible as the Word of God has the same characteristic as any human word, that is to say, it remains fully and truly the word of the speaker and expresses his mind, whether or not it is understood or even listened to. If it takes the form of a command, the Word of God is to be obeyed even though the hearer does not acknowledge its Author, and if the form of a promise, it is to be trusted even though it is not listened to. This is because it is the Word of God addressed to all those of whom he is the gracious Creator. But (and in this respect, too, it is just like any human word) the Bible as the Word of God does not establish a personal relationship with the speaker unless there is a glad response by the hearer. When it is heard in this way it authenticates itself to the hearer as being the word of the speaker, in the same way as any human word does.

Since it is the Word of God, Scripture is self-authenticating to those who receive it. It authenticates itself to the Christian heart. We hand it on as God's Word to those who come after us, just as we ourselves received it from those who went before us,[12] having for ourselves found it to be God's Word, in which God speaks to us, and through which we have fellowship with him.

This conviction may be tested for its reasonableness and its truth by other considerations. For example, our contemporaries, whose spirituality we know, lend their testimony to our own experience that the same spiritual experiences as ours are theirs through reading the Scriptures. Great saints, whose religious views are of the weightiest, have affirmed God's relationship to Scripture. Such are Paul

12 2 Tim 1:13-14, 2:1-2

and Peter. Jesus Christ himself testified that the Scripture received by his fellow Jews was indeed the Word of God. Furthermore, the perceived character of Scripture confirms its divine origin. The loftiness of its religious and ethical teaching, its consistency with itself throughout its pages, though composed over a period of a millennium, and the rationality of its world view—all confirm the reasonableness of the conviction that the true God has spoken and speaks to us through the Bible.

God is in his Word. He is in it not only when the Bible is read, but also when it is truly preached, or witnessed to, or reflected on in the mind; we meet him in it, and so his Word brings both knowledge and fellowship.

The character of Scripture

The Word of God will have certain characteristics because of its authorship. Not only will it be infallible and inerrant in what it is saying to us, but it will be effective in its purposes, so that those to whom it is addressed will hear it and be able to understand it; that is to say, it will be perspicuous. These characteristics of God's Word spring from its Author. We are not able to say the same of our own words, which are fallible through our ignorance and sin. Moreover, our words may not be heard by those to whom we address them, and may not be understood, even when heard, because of our inability to express ourselves clearly. None of these things is true of the divine Word. It is effective; it accomplishes the purpose for which it is sent; it is heard by those to whom it is addressed. It authenticates itself as God's Word in the hearts of those who hear it. It is perspicuous and understandable and, of course, it is true, reliable, infallible, inerrant in what it is telling us.

This puts the Word of God into a classification quite distinct and different from all other words that we may hear. People's words share all the defects of our sinful imperfect nature, but God's Word is altogether different. It is perfect, whether spoken by God directly, or through prophets, or by the incarnate Son of God, or by the inspired writers of Scripture. For us, the only Word of God that we have is this last, the Holy Scripture. We are not in a position to leave our job to go out to listen to Jesus speaking on the hills of Galilee. We do not hear God addressing us directly from heaven as did those assembled in the church at the rock of Horeb,[13] nor are there prophets in our midst who are able to say with truth, "Thus saith the Lord". We do, however, have Holy Scripture which Peter himself said is more sure than even his own memory of the Galilean ministry of Jesus.[14]

The canon

The giving by God of his Word in written form immediately brings into being the concept of the canon, because God's Word, with its perfections, is set in a category of writing quite distinct from all other writings. God's Word is normative for our life. It is authoritative over our conscience. The words of our fellow men are not so. God's Word is perfect; our writings are imperfect. The canon then is a very simple concept. It is putting into one classification or pigeon-hole those writings of which God is the Author, and putting into the other pigeon-hole all

13 Deut 18:16
14 2 Pet 1:19; cf. Greek.

other writings which people have written—with a greater or lesser degree of truth—but which are not written by the direct inspiration of the Holy Spirit to convey God's mind and Word to the reader, and are consequently not authoritative over the conscience.

The canon is a simple concept, although the exact extent of it may sometimes be a cause for investigation and reflection. But the simple concept of the canon is confused today in theological circles, and the reason is easy to find. Theologians have denied the unique character of the scriptural writings. The Scriptures are now widely regarded as merely the record of God's Word and not as themselves being God's direct and infallible Word. If Scripture is only another form of human writing and not primarily divine, the concept of the canon evaporates. There are no longer two clearly distinct varieties of books that we may read—one of which God is the Author, and the other of which men and women are the authors. But now all are included in the one category; all are only human writings, and this is what many modern theologians affirm. No wonder, then, that the concept of the canon is in confusion, for the word 'canon' means a rule or measuring rod. It is the standard by which things are judged. Naturally in religious and moral matters, indeed in everything, God's Word, if we have it, is automatically the canon, and there is no other canon or standard of measurement which can compare to the Word of God. But if there is no clear Word of God, then there is no canon to rule thought, faith and conduct.

Given the view of Scripture held by many modern writers, there can be no such thing as canonicity; but this is not always realized. So all sorts of variations of the old and simple concept of the canon are held. For example, the idea of a canon within the canon has been aired, but how this can be is hard to understand. A writing is either canonical, that is to say, God's Word, and so of normative authority over life, or it is not canonical, being man's word, and however good and inspiring and helpful and true, cannot rule the conscience in the way that God's Word must. The phrase 'a canon within the canon' is used to assess canonicity by the quality of the message of a book. This is altogether too subjective and imposes our concepts on the Holy Spirit of prophecy. We cannot restrict the Holy Spirit to certain themes, as though we knew the whole mosaic of the revelation which the Spirit intends to give us. Prophecy is the only possible criterion for canonicity.

The view of the Bible current among many New Testament scholars and theologians is that it is not prophecy—that is, it is not God's Word written, but that it is a record of God's revelation, in particular, that it is a record of his revelation in Christ, who is supremely the Word of God. This modern view of the Bible suffers from many defects which render it untenable. It is contradictory to the views of Jesus himself. He regarded the written Word of Scripture as God's Word spoken in the past to the present readers. "Have you not read", he asked the Sadducees, "that which was spoken to you by God?" Secondly, it is contrary to the Nicene Creed, which states that the Holy Spirit spoke by the prophets—a reference to the prophetic writings of Scripture; so that the existence of a canon or body of authoritative prophetic writing is an article of the Christian faith.

The Bible the Word of God

The statement of the creed is based on the testimony of Scripture itself and in particular on the testimony of Jesus Christ who regarded the Bible as God's infallible Word.[15] He had plainly studied it thoroughly before his ministry began. He quoted it in reply to the temptations of the devil and asserted that our life is to be based on every word that proceeds from the mouth of God.[16] The whole of the written Scripture was regarded by Jesus as spoken by God. For example, in Matthew 19:5 Jesus quoted a comment of the writer of Genesis and attributed this comment to God himself. The writer to the Hebrews has the same view. In Hebrews 3:7 a verse from the Old Testament is introduced by the words "as the Holy Spirit says". The writer realized that though the verse was written by the psalmist, the real Author was God. Similarly in Acts 1:16, the quotation from the Bible is introduced by the phrase "the Scripture… which the Holy Ghost foretold by the mouth of David". (There are very similar words in Acts 4:25.) This is an interesting illustration of the two-sided truth that David wrote the words of the psalm naturally and freely, drawing on his experience, yet the true Author was the Holy Spirit who was infallibly directing those faculties which he himself had given to David.

There are many other illustrations of this New Testament attitude to Holy Scripture. Consequently the creed is right in affirming that the Holy Spirit spoke by the prophets and we should not circumscribe this reference to the

15 John 10:35
16 Matt 4:4

prophets to mean simply those writers whom we call prophets, for it extends to the whole of prophetic Scripture, to 'every prophecy of Scripture', to use the phraseology of 2 Peter 1:20. The New Testament Scriptures are also included. Romans 16:26 is evidence of a body of New Testament prophetic Scripture received by the apostolic church. Paul explicitly stated that his own letters were prophetic Scripture and fully canonical.[17] He cited Luke's Gospel as Scripture,[18] and spoke generally of the revelation of the mystery of Christ, revealed through the apostles and New Testament prophets, among which he included his own writings.[19]

All of Paul's Epistles are included in Holy Scripture in 2 Peter 3:16. Consequently, we ought not to restrict 2 Timothy 3:16—"All Scripture is inspired by God"—to the Old Testament, because at the time this was written there were New Testament Scriptures acknowledged and accepted in the Christian fellowship.

The existence of a canon of prophetic writings of Old and New Testament is an article of the Christian faith, taught clearly in the New Testament and affirmed Sunday by Sunday in the creed.

A third objection to the modern view, which regards the Bible not as God's Word written but only as a record of God's Word, is that it prevents the Bible from doing its proper work in convicting the conscience and so moving the will of the reader to obedience. God's Word rules the conscience,

17 1 Cor 14:37
18 1 Tim 5:18
19 Eph 3:3-5

but a human record can never attain to this normative or canonical status. When the Bible is accepted as God's Word written, the preacher's task, though not easy, is simple in concept. He is to make clear to the eager listener what the Bible is teaching, and the conscience of the hearer gladly responds in obedience and faith to that Word of God clearly seen in the Bible through the preacher's exposition.

If, however, the Bible is primarily a human record of God's revelation in the past, it cannot evoke this spontaneous response in the regenerate heart of the listener. Human words must be assessed as to whether they are true and ought to be followed. For it is always possible that the record, if only human, is erroneous. Consequently, on the modern view that the Bible is a human record, the preacher's task has radically changed. Instead of expounding clearly the Word of God and enjoining it on the conscience of God's children to be trusted and obeyed, he is simply putting before his hearers ideas which they may treat as they like, according to their own judgement and assessment. In short, the preacher's distinctive ministry has disappeared if the Bible is not the Word of God. Could the reason why many clergy are uncertain about their role, and why they do not make public and private preaching and teaching their primary ministry, be that they doubt the infallibility of the Bible and so have lost their canon?

It is essential to hold firmly to the view of Jesus and the apostles that the written Scripture is God's Word, and therefore that we must believe it with joy, submit to it and obey it with alacrity and single-mindedness, so that its glorious promises set our standard of values and suffuse our life with hope.

chapter 2

God of infinite power, wisdom and goodness[1]

God is of infinite power. The notion of power is contained in the notion of deity. Wherever people believe in God (and this belief is as universal as the human race), God (or the gods) is thought of as powerful. However, the concept of *infinite and unlimited* power is not generally attributed to the gods of paganism, yet it is clearly affirmed of the true and living God of Holy Scripture. "Nothing is too hard for the Lord" is a refrain that runs through Scripture.[2] It was the sheet-anchor of Jesus' ministry. He told his despairing disciples, as they realized the difficulty of anyone being saved, that what was impossible with people is possible with God,[3] and in that last agonizing prayer in the garden of Gethsemane, he based his request on the completeness of God's power. "Abba, Father, all things are possible to you".[4]

Two thousand years earlier, when the divine messenger had brought Abraham and Sarah the good news that Sarah would bear a son, although humanly speaking this was a physical impossibility, the assurance was given that 'Nothing

1 This phrase is taken from the first of the Thirty-nine Articles of Religion of the Church of England, which begins: "There is but one living and true God, everlasting, without body, parts, or passions; of infinite power, wisdom and goodness; the Maker, and Preserver of all things both visible and invisible".
2 For example, Genesis 18:14; Job 42:2.
3 Matt 19:26
4 Mark 14:36

is too hard for Yahweh',[5] and so it came about.[6] When Jeremiah was faced with the apparent contradiction of on the one hand God's purpose in the destruction of Jerusalem, and on the other the word that came to him to buy a block of land in Judah, he cast himself onto God with the prayer, "Ah Lord Yahweh! Behold, you have made the heavens and the earth by your great power and by your outstretched arm! *Nothing is too difficult for you*... You have said to me, O Lord Yahweh, 'Buy for yourself the field for money, and call in witnesses'—although the city is given into the hand of the Chaldeans."

Yahweh replied, "Behold I am Yahweh, the God of all flesh, *is anything too difficult for me?*... Behold, I am about to give this city into the hand of the Chaldeans... [but] behold, I will gather them out of all the lands to which I have driven them in my anger... and I will bring them back to this place and make them dwell in safety".[7] And so it came about. There is nothing too hard for Yahweh. As Job exclaimed, "I know that you can do all things, and that no purpose of yours can be thwarted".[8] The virgin Mary received the same assurance from the angel Gabriel in response to her natural enquiry as to how it could be that the promise of a son should be fulfilled to her who had no husband. "For nothing will be

5 Textual note: In the original edition of *The Everlasting God*, the author used Jehovah as the traditional English transliteration of the Hebrew name of God (the 'YHWH' that is rendered in most English Bibles as 'the LORD'). In this edition, it has been rendered as 'Yahweh'. It must be acknowledged that 'Yahweh' is not a certain translation, but it is more likely to be accurate than 'Jehovah' and less confusing to the reader than 'LORD'.

6 Gen 18:14

7 Jer 32:15-37

8 Job 42:2

impossible with God".[9]

The true and living God has revealed himself as a God of infinite power. The only things impossible to him are those which contradict his character. He cannot lie, he cannot change, he cannot cease from being good.[10]

Creation

The clearest example of God's power is the act of creation. All that we see around us is the result of God's creative power. The universe came into being through his Word, "For he commanded and they were created" as the psalmist put it.[11] The concept that God created everything out of nothing is fundamental to the Scripture and is found throughout its pages. The God of Holy Scripture, the God of revelation, is the Creator God, the God of infinite power. Nor did his powerful acts cease with creation, but he controls what he created. His infinite mind controls absolutely, all the time, every detail of created things. We find this thought a difficulty, but it ought not to be so, for we believe that we have evidence that our own minds to a limited extent may sometimes be able to influence matter, even though it is not created by us. God's infinite mind controls everything and he can as easily alter it at any moment as create it in the first place. God spoke and it was done, and God's Word continues to have the same infinite power. Whatever he wills comes to pass, and nothing comes to pass except in accordance with what he wills. Chance and luck are non-existent. They are

9 Luke 1:37
10 For example, Titus 1:2; Malachi 3:6.
11 Ps 148:5; cf. Ps 33:5-9

simply words to describe that which is unforeseeable by us.

The Bible puts before us a consistent world view based on the infinite power of God. Thus Jesus said that God makes the sun to rise and sends the rain.[12] In saying this Jesus is simply repeating the consistent teaching of Scripture that the natural phenomena are the direct results of God's will, whether there are rain and fruitful seasons, or whether there is a drought. Our minds have difficulty with this. We see only the proximate causes (the meteorological laws as we call them) or the laws of cause and effect. But it is the mind of God which gives all these laws their motive force. It is God who makes the sun to rise. It is God who raises up the stormy wind.[13] It is God who makes the storm to cease.[14] It was God who sent the flood.

After the flood God promised Noah in the covenant with creation recorded in Genesis 9 that his dealings with the world would be on the basis of consistency, that seed-time and harvest, cold and heat, summer and winter, day and night would not cease so long as the world lasts. This consistency is part of the purpose of God, for without it human life as we know it could not be sustained. If, for example, there were no consistency in the seasons, we could neither sow nor reap. But this consistency of God's working must not be mistaken for an inevitable and inexorable law of cause and effect. Ultimately, God is the only cause, and it is his mind and will which cause all things. God wills consistency, and that is why we experience consistency.

12 Matt 5:45
13 Ps 107:25
14 Ps 107:29

Although we speak of the laws of nature governing physical events, this is a misnomer. The laws of nature are not laws in the true sense but are observed consistencies of sequences of past events. They do not govern the future. God's consistent mind governs the future as he has governed the observed past.

If in his wisdom God wills that an event in nature should differ from the unbroken sequence before or after (for example, that the sun should stand still), then it will differ.[15] We shall call it a miracle. Others who do not know God's power will deny that it happened. But there is no reason for this denial. Since God is a free Person we cannot lay down in advance how he will create the world or how he will order events within it. We know that he is loving, righteous and holy in all he does, but we cannot know the mind of the Lord for physical phenomena. Experience is our only source of this knowledge.

However, since God is a God of order and faithfulness, it is possible to develop the discipline of natural science. For science works through prediction based on precedent, that is, on the observed sequences of the past, 'the customs of the Creator'. We call these customs of the Creator natural laws. But God's will is the basis of each event. However, since God has linked events in 'causal' chains, it is possible to understand the whole series of events without reference to God. God is an unnecessary hypothesis for science, but not for the reflective scientist. For it is not a contradiction, but rather a necessary element of the whole concept, to realize that every 'cause' in the chain has the will of God as its own

15 Josh 10:12-13

underlying and true cause. God holds all things together and in them he is working all things after the counsel of his own will.[16]

The doctrine of God the Creator is vivid throughout the pages of Scripture. The gods of the nations are not creator gods and, as the interesting little Aramaic insertion in Jeremiah puts it, the gods that did not create the world will perish, as indeed they have.[17] In our own times idolatry, which was a universal substitute for the Creator God, has been replaced by the widely held theory of evolution. Both are substitutes for the concept of the Creator God. Just as the ancients and the heathen today deified and worshipped the creature as the creator, modelling images of man or birds or animals or reptiles and worshipping these, so for Western secular people the modern theory of evolution deifies nature and acknowledges it as creator of all we see around us. All the beauty and intricacy and all the marvellous arrangements of the natural world are supposed to have been evolved by a thoughtless, purposeless, mechanical operation of nature, and in this way the God who made the world is as effectively shut out of the minds of those who are enjoying the blessings of his creation as he was by the false religions of idolatry. Just as the idolaters could not see the foolishness, indeed the stupidity, of worshipping gods of wood and stone, which have no life nor purpose nor mind, so modern believers in the theory of evolution cannot see the foolishness of that theory, which not only lacks evidence to support it, but also runs counter to such evidence of origins

16 Eph 1:11; Col 1:17
17 Jer 10:11

as is available. Nevertheless, this false world view is being indoctrinated into children in the schools with the aid of public money and placarded in natural history museums as though it were the only explanation of the world around us, while those who criticize and expose the theory receive the same intense religious hostility as did those who denounced idolatry in earlier days. The Bible says that if we refuse to have the Creator God in our mind, God gives us up to a reprobate mind.[18]

God's infinite power controls what he has created. We have seen that Jesus taught that the phenomena of nature are under God's control. That is why we may pray for favourable weather. To describe the weather as under God's control is not mere poetry, but a direct description of the facts. It may not be God's will to alter the consistent way by which he regulates the weather—a consistency which we call meteorological laws—yet it may be his gracious will to accede to our request. When he does this, he will do it in what we would call a natural way, but the one who prayed will know the real reason why the weather changed.

God's control over evil wills

God's control over his creation extends to control over the wills of people. Sinful people are within this complete control of God, otherwise sin would be a marvellous achievement, if by it we could remove ourselves from God's sovereign and absolute power. But it is not so. The brigands who slaughtered Job's servants and carried off his cattle were as much under the control of God, although they did

18 Rom 1:18-28

not know it, as was the wind that destroyed the house in which Job's children were gathered.[19] Job acknowledged this by his pious and true reaction to the tragic news: "Yahweh gave, and Yahweh has taken away; blessed be the name of Yahweh".[20] Ultimately, it was Yahweh who took away Job's possessions and his children. Although the agents were men and spirits of an evil and malevolent character, yet they were not outside God's control and were operating within the sphere of his perfect will and purposes. They originated the evil, but they were not able to act contrary to what God willed should come to pass. Similarly, in Isaiah 10 the prophet recounts how the Assyrians are the rod of God's anger. Those cruel armies invading Palestine were the instruments of a well-deserved judgement. Yet the Assyrians were totally unaware that they were acting under God's control and fulfilling his purpose. They attributed their success to their military prowess, but the prophet foretold that their cruelties would in due course receive retribution, just as Israel had experienced judgement through them.

Centuries before, Joseph had reassured his brothers that his captivity in Egypt was part of God's perfect will to bless: "God sent me before you to preserve for you a remnant... and to keep you alive by a great deliverance. Now, therefore, it was not you that sent me here, but God."[21] Again, a little later, he once more reassured them with the words: "As for you, you meant evil against me; but God meant it for good in order to bring about this present result, to preserve many

19 Job 1:13-19
20 Job 1:21
21 Gen 45:7-8

people alive".[22] It must have been a great source of strength to Joseph throughout the bitter years of his imprisonment to realize that God was sovereign over every event in the experiences which he was suffering. Nothing takes place in God's creation apart from God's will because God is of infinite power.

The doctrine of God's absolute and complete providence and control over every event is a ground for banishing fear from the hearts of the people of God. Thus Jesus reminded his disciples, "Are not five sparrows sold for two cents? And yet not one of them is forgotten before God. Indeed, the very hairs of your head are all numbered. Do not fear; you are of more value than many sparrows."[23] In the Old Testament the doctrine of God's sovereignty is the comfort and strength of his people. Thus through the prophet Isaiah God says, "I, even I, am he that comforts you. Who are you that you are afraid of man who dies, and of the son of man who is made like grass; that you have forgotten Yahweh your Maker, who stretched out the heavens and laid the foundations of the earth?"[24]

The creative power of God which brought all things into being is the guarantee that he is able to sustain us in every detail of life. The doctrine of creation is basic to the Christian doctrine of God.

The infinite power and the infinite mind of God, to which the marvels of creation bear witness, mean that he is able to give full attention, care and protection to every

22 Gen 50:20
23 Luke 12:6-7
24 Isa 51:12-13

person throughout the world with the same intensity of concern that he would give if he were related to a single individual only. The infinity of God is not overwhelmed by numbers, nor stupefied by detail. God is able to comprehend, and provide for at the same time, the needs of the whole of his creation. Our heavenly Father gives each of us his undivided attention and his full friendship as though we were his only friend.

Purpose and judgement

Creation implies purpose. In contrast, impersonal evolution is purposeless—things happening by accident without plan. But creation is a personal activity of an almighty, supreme God. Personal action implies purpose, and this in turn implies assessment. The doctrine of judgement is closely related to that of creation. The Scriptures are full of the truth of the judgement of God. One of the oldest passages of the Old Testament, the song of Deborah, proclaims how turning away from the true God brought inevitable judgement: "New gods were chosen; then war was in the gates".[25] The events in the historical books of the Old Testament underscore the truth that judgement follows wrongdoing. The main theme of the prophets is the inevitability of judgement unless God's people return and seek God's forgiveness in repentance. A passage from Jeremiah will illustrate this. Jeremiah is told by the Lord to write in a book his prophecies "from the day I first spoke to you, from the days of Josiah even to this day. Perhaps the house of Judah will hear all the calamity which I plan to

25 Judg 5:8

bring on them, in order that every man will turn from his evil way; that I will forgive their iniquity and their sin."[26] Judgement is inevitable. The purpose of God's making it known to us is that we might repent and amend our lives in the light of the inevitability of this future assessment, and so escape judgement.

The theme of judgement is as prominent in the New Testament as in the Old. Jesus spoke much about the doom of outer darkness, where there is weeping and gnashing of teeth in hopeless remorse, and also of hell (or Gehenna), where the worm does not die and the fire is never put out.[27] He warned his hearers not to fear people who might put to death the body, but to fear God who could destroy both body and soul in hell.[28] Again, speaking to the Jewish leaders, he said, "You serpents, you brood of vipers, how shall you escape the sentence of hell?"[29]

Judgement was an integral part of Paul's message. He wrote in Romans 2 of "the day when, according to my gospel, God will judge the secrets of men through Jesus Christ".[30] When preaching in the market-place at Athens, his sermon reached its climax as he proclaimed that God has fixed the judgement day when he will judge the world in righteousness by the Man whom he has chosen and he has given proof of this by raising him from the dead.[31] A final illustration from Paul will underline this point still more clearly. When Paul was a prisoner in Caesarea and had the

26 Jer 36:2-3
27 Matt 8:12, 22:13, 25:30; Mark 9:43-44
28 Matt 10:28
29 Matt 23:33
30 Rom 2:16
31 Acts 17:31

opportunity of preaching before Governor Felix, at Felix's request, he spoke about faith in Jesus Christ, "discussing righteousness, self-control and the judgement to come".[32] This summary of perhaps Paul's most significant sermon shows how central was judgement in the Christian gospel. In his second letter to the Thessalonians, Paul described this "manifest judgement of God" in most vivid terms. He wrote:

> For after all it is only just for God to repay with affliction those who afflict you, and to give relief to you who are afflicted and to us as well when the Lord Jesus shall be revealed from heaven with his mighty angels in flaming fire, dealing out retribution to those who do not know God and to those who do not obey the gospel of our Lord Jesus. And these will pay the penalty of eternal destruction, away from the presence of the Lord and from the glory of his power, when he comes to be glorified in his saints on that day, and to be marvelled at among all who have believed—for our testimony to you was believed.[33]

The phrase 'that day' was well understood by New Testament Christians to stand for the judgement day. It is a common New Testament phrase because judgement is a common New Testament concept.

Judgement is a central theme of the book of Revelation and is displayed vividly in a series of pictures, so that it might have its proper influence on the conscience and the will of believers.

32 Acts 24:24-25
33 2 Thess 1:6-10

Judgement will be thorough and complete. Jesus said that we will give an account of every idle word.[34] Idle words are perhaps the least significant of any of our actions, yet they will not escape God's assessment. God is infinite and his judgement will take into account everything, even every idle word.

The Bible is clear that God's judgement will be righteous, that is to say, it will be absolutely just and fair. The statement that God will render to every person according to their works runs like a refrain through both Old and New Testaments.[35] The righteous judgement of God is a consolation to his people when they are suffering wrongfully at the hands of their enemies, for God will repay, and repay righteously.[36] They will be vindicated. On the other hand the righteous judgement of God is an awful subject for sinners to contemplate. It is a fearful thing to fall into the hand of the living God.[37]

A gospel which contains judgement as a prominent strand, as does the New Testament gospel, is relevant to men and women everywhere and in every age and culture. It does not need indigenization,[38] so popular a catchword today, but requires only clarity of language and faithfulness in proclamation. The sense of right and wrong is universal in the human race and so is the knowledge that we fall below our own standards of what is right, and that this entails death. Thus the gospel that contains judgement, and

34 Matt 12:36
35 1 Sam 26:23; Prov 24:12; Rom 2:6; Rev 22:12
36 Isa 59:17-20; Deut 7:9-10
37 Heb 10:31
38 The more current term now would be 'contextualization'.

salvation from judgement, is a gospel that is always relevant to the hearer, no matter to what stage of civilization he may have attained. Such a gospel does not need to be assimilated to the culture of the people who are hearing it. A theology that proclaims the God who saves from judgement by forgiveness through faith in the Lord Jesus Christ does not need to be adapted for Australian audiences, or to be turned into a black theology for the blacks of North America. Asian Christians and Western Christians need the same gospel and the same theology which is based on it, and all are able to understand it, no matter how different the cultural backgrounds of the hearers and preachers may be, so long as the proclamation is true to the New Testament gospel of judgement and salvation from judgement.

A gospel that minimizes or omits judgement must concentrate on this life and the benefits that Christ brings for this life. Most modern preaching, whether liberal or evangelical, falls into this mistake. The liberal preacher may emphasize a social gospel, for example, one of alleviation of poverty or political oppression; the evangelical may emphasize a happy life, love, joy and forgiveness.

But the Christian gospel is concerned with the future. It proclaims Jesus who rescues us from the wrath to come.[39] When hearers accept the gospel for the benefits of this life, such as peace and happiness, it is a contradiction to ask them to suffer for the gospel. The whole purpose of their accepting the gospel was for some present benefit which they had been offered by the preacher. This presentation and acceptance of the gospel of Jesus Christ for benefits it brings

39 1 Thess 1:10

here and now may well be the explanation of why it is that although evangelical Christianity is growing, for example in the United States, Christian influence on society is receding. There may be more true Christians in the community, nevertheless the forces of evil—as reflected, for example, in the increase of drunkenness, gambling, permissiveness, sexual immorality and dishonesty in business—continue to grow, in spite of the preaching of the gospel and the conversion of men and women to Christ. What is required, if we are to maintain a true spiritual witness against social evils, is the willingness to suffer for the sake of the truth. Such willingness to suffer will only be created by a gospel that proclaims a future judgement and a salvation from that judgement through forgiveness and justification in Christ, so that our thoughts are fixed on that future rather than on some present blessing for which we may have embraced the gospel and which is threatened by suffering. Christians today are like salt that has lost its savour, through loss of heavenly-mindedness.[40]

The modern gospel does not draw tears from the preacher as he preaches. Yet it is a characteristic of the New Testament gospel that the preacher was moved to tears. For example, our Lord wept over Jerusalem.[41] The tears were drawn out, not because Jerusalem was missing out on some present blessing, but rather because it was neglecting its opportunity of repentance and so of salvation from the inevitable future judgement when its enemies would come upon it and not leave one stone upon another, a judgement

40 Matt 5:13; Col 3:1-4
41 Matt 23:37ff.; Luke 19:41-44

too awful to contemplate, a tribulation such as had never occurred in the history of the world before. Paul, too, wept over the impenitent. In Romans 9 he testified that he had constant pain in his heart through the unbelief of his kinsmen. In Acts 20, Paul, giving a summary of his three years' ministry at Ephesus, mentioned twice over that his preaching was accompanied by tears. Tears in the preacher are evoked by deeply felt sympathy with the predicament of those who are listening, a predicament which the preacher shares but from which he has been rescued by the gospel which he is bringing. When that gospel is rejected, tears are drawn from the preacher as he earnestly seeks the good of those to whom he has been sent. Our modern gospel does not evoke tears in the preacher because the dimension of judgement has almost completely been eliminated. A gospel without tears, because without judgement, is not the gospel of the New Testament.

Judgement is prominent in the biblical message. But the Bible has to be believed without wavering if judgement is to be prominent in preaching which at the same time is compassionate preaching. It is easy for a preacher, lacking sympathy with the human race, to throw brickbats of judgement at the heads of his hearers. On the other hand, since the world does not believe in judgement nor like to hear of it, a considerate preacher will avoid the subject unless, unshaken by private doubts, he remains firm in his belief in the reliability and truth of God's Word, which is so full of judgement.

Creation and judgement are the focal points around which human life moves. These two truths, closely related because they both spring from a supreme purposeful Creator, should not be far from the thoughts of any. They are central in the Christian gospel, but neither purposeful creation nor future assessment finds any place in the alternative explanation of reality which the modern world embraces and which goes by the name of evolution.

Everlasting, without body, parts or passions

God is everlasting, without body, parts or passions. These phrases from the first of the Thirty-nine Articles simply draw out the thought that is contained within the concept of deity. Everlastingness, infinity in time, is inherent in the notion of deity. Humanity is conscious that its life is temporary, but the gods have always been thought of as immortal. Consequently, the epithet 'everlasting' simply draws out what is contained in the word 'God' and what is thoroughly endorsed by the Bible, which terms God "the everlasting God".[42]

At first sight, in view of numerous passages of Scripture, it might seem strange to deny God a body, but a body is a form of limitation. God is not limited by externals; he is infinite. He is not limited as we are by location. He is omnipresent, present equally everywhere; but ubiquity is contradictory to the concept of a body. The scriptural descriptions of God in bodily terms, such as the eyes of the Lord, or the right hand, are metaphors.

'Without parts' is inherent in the concept of spirit. God is spirit and spirit is not composite, made up of parts as material objects are. Spirit is not divisible. Jesus taught

42 Gen 21:33; Isa 40:28

that God is spirit.[43] Our knowledge of spirit comes from our knowledge of ourselves. We know we are an indivisible unity.

'Without passions' does not mean that God is without feeling, but it means that God is not subject to control from outside himself. He is not passive, he is not the recipient, willy-nilly, of the action of others, but he is the One on whom all activity depends. For he is sovereign; he is of infinite power.

Of infinite goodness

God is of infinite goodness. Goodness may be defined as concern for other people's welfare, that is, interest in others and the desire and activity of promoting their welfare. The Scriptures constantly affirm that God is good.[44] Creation exhibits the goodness of God in a very clear manner. As the Scripture says, God saw the creation that it was very good.[45] He created the world to be inhabited,[46] and its inhabitants enjoy living within the created world. The world is beautiful and we enjoy its beauty. The tourist industry witnesses to the pleasures of beauty that are built into the creation. The whole of life in its created nature is pleasant to live. For example, it is pleasant to eat and without eating we would not survive! The world brings pleasure to the creature.

This ought to evoke thanksgiving to the Creator. Thanksgiving is a duty, and like all natural duties, it too is pleasant, for it increases the experience of the pleasure, by

43 John 4:24
44 Ps 100:5; Mark 10:18
45 Gen 1:31
46 Isa 45:18

minimizing self-centredness and sharing the joy, for shared joys are deepened. But as Paul says in Romans 1, this basic primary response of thanksgiving is where humanity fails and, failing at this point, the whole relationship with God is brought into jeopardy.

Goodness in relationship involves responsibility

The act of creation brings the Creator into a relationship of responsibility for the welfare of his creation. For otherwise God would not be good. From the moment of creation the good God is in a relationship of care and concern for that which he has brought into being, and his care and concern are infinite and never vary or fail. In a word we may say that God is in a covenant relationship with his creation from the inception of its existence. In the true world, where goodness is basic, creation involves covenant. God has always been and will always be in covenant relationship with his creation and, since God is good, the covenant is always a covenant of grace. Its character and content will vary with humanity's situation and need.

The covenant, implicit in creation, becomes explicit in Genesis 6 and 9. In these passages, God promises that he will maintain his covenant. "I will maintain my covenant with you and with your seed after you and with every living creature that is with you."[47] The word 'maintain' indicates that the covenant was already in existence, confirming that the fact of covenant is involved in the act of creation by the good Creator. The terms of this covenant are that God will

47 Gen 9:9-10

maintain the stability of the earth in order that humanity's life might prosper. There will be no more cataclysms; there will be no irregularity in the seasons but while the earth remains, seed-time and harvest, cold and heat, summer and winter, day and night shall not cease. This is God's promise and this is God's fulfilment. The consistency of the natural phenomena is the basis of human life. We can rely upon the future and so take action in the present with a view to that future. This is part of the goodness of God. As Paul put it, he fills our hearts with food and gladness through sending us fruitful seasons.[48]

God's covenant relationship with creation, when expressed in personal terms, means that he is faithful; he fulfils that which he promises. He is the faithful God and we are to reflect his faithfulness in our relationships, not only with God, but with one another. The virtue of faithfulness must not be degraded into loyalty. Although this word has begun to appear in modern English versions of the Bible, loyalty is not a biblical notion, and is often the cause of grave injustice. But faithfulness is always a virtue and a duty. In Scripture, God is described as the faithful God.[49] The faithfulness of God is the most important aspect of his goodness. Without this divine attribute of faithfulness it would not be possible to practise the Christian religion, because the Christian religion is a relationship with God, a relationship with a God who can be trusted, a relationship which calls for the response of obedience and hope. Now obedience and hope are based on the knowledge of God's

48 Acts 14:17
49 Deut 7:9, 32:4

faithfulness. It is because God, who has promised, is faithful that we gladly obey him in the way that he has directed in order to attain his sure promises. The goodness of God and his covenant relationship with all that he has created are expressed in Psalm 104. The wildlife of the jungle and of the open countryside look to God for the provision of their daily food. As Jesus said, the sparrows are fed by him; how much more men and women, whom he created in his own image for fellowship with himself?[50]

Responsibility involves authority

Because God is responsible for our welfare, he has authority over us. Authority and responsibility go hand in hand. Those who receive benefit from the exercise of responsibility have the obligation to respond by obedience to the authority within the area of its responsibility. This is true, not only in relation to God, but in all areas of human life. Thus the state has responsibility for the welfare of the citizens in the areas of justice and virtue, and therefore has authority over the citizens within those areas. It is the duty of the citizens to respond with obedience, thanksgiving and honour. Similarly, in the family it is the duty of the parents, and particularly of the father, to advance the welfare of all the members of the family while they are still dependent. He must take thought and action for their benefit. Consequently, he has authority within the area of that responsibility. If he acts beyond his responsibility, then his authority ceases at that point. But within the area of his responsibility he has authority, and consequently there is an obligation on those who benefit

50 Matt 6:26, 10:29-31

from his care and concern to obey him, within the area of his authority and also to be thankful for the thoughtfulness and for the action taken on their behalf and for their benefit.

Obligation to obey ceases when commands are given beyond the area of responsibility. An illustration is Peter's refusal to obey the Jewish authorities. They were giving commands which were contrary to the commands of God.[51] But since the authority of rulers is a delegated authority as the ministers of God,[52] when they give commands which contradict God's commands, they have exceeded their responsibility of being God's ministers. Yet a command that appears to be unjust to oneself may not necessarily be outside the area of responsibility and consequently is to be obeyed, as Peter reminded those unfortunate slaves who had unjust masters.[53]

Closely related to obedience and thanksgiving is honour. We are to give honour to those in authority—give recognition, that is, to their authoritative position, an authority which derives from their relationship with us of responsibility for our welfare. The obligation to honour continues even when the responsibility has been fulfilled and the authority has ceased.

God's relationship to us is one of complete responsibility for all aspects of our life and therefore his authority is complete. We on our part must recognize the authority which accompanies this responsibility by giving complete and absolute obedience to God. There is no area of our life

51 Acts 5:29
52 Rom 13:4
53 1 Pet 2:18

which is outside his responsibility, and since he is a good God he is active in discharging that responsibility for our welfare. Therefore we are to obey him in everything, to be thankful to him in everything, to honour him in everything.

God is of infinite power, but power in itself does not confer authority. God's power has brought us into being through creation, but his power alone is not the ground of our obligation to obey him. The ground of that obligation is his goodness coupled with his power, for his goodness means that he is concerned for the welfare of his creation and his power enables him to give effect to this concern. As the infinitely good Creator, he accepts responsibility for the welfare of his creation; that is, he is in covenant relationship with it. He is actively promoting its welfare, and this relationship of real responsibility confers authority and calls for the response of obedience from those who benefit, for this is their acknowledgement of the relationship.

First, there is the relationship, then there is the responsibility of that relationship. From this flows the authority which God has over all, and which leads in turn to the obligation on all of obedience, thanksgiving and honour. In short, goodness in relationship plus ability to discharge the responsibilities of that relationship are the ground for authority, not only in the affairs of humans but also in the ultimate relationship of God and his creation.

We may apply this concept to the life of the congregation and ask, 'Who has authority within the congregation?' We answer, 'Only those who rightly have responsibility for the spiritual welfare of the congregation, and only to the extent of their responsibility'. Those who benefit from the exercise of the responsibility, with its care, concern and thoughtfulness for the benefit of the recipients, are obliged not only to honour the authority, but also to obey it within the area of its responsibility, but not beyond. If authority is exercised beyond that area of responsibility it becomes usurped authority and carries no obligation for obedience. We all have responsibility for the welfare of fellow members of the congregation and to this extent we are all to submit to one another, as Paul commanded the Ephesians.[54] But some members because of their recognized gifts have greater responsibility and so greater authority, which other members have the duty to acknowledge and to obey.[55]

God's infinite power coupled with his infinite goodness mean that he is not niggardly in conferring benefits on his creation. He is not, for example, like the gods of the ancient civilizations, who were thought to be envious of the prosperity of humans; but God loves his creation, cares for it and bestows blessings on it with a generous hand. As the Scripture says, "No good thing does he withhold from those that walk uprightly";[56] and again, "In your right hand there are pleasures forever".[57] As Paul said, God "richly supplies us with all things to enjoy".[58] God's goodness means that he is other-person-centred. He has created us in his image to be other-person-centred. In Jesus we have been given the example and pattern of how we should use the good things he gives us by sharing them with others. Our Lord himself has told us that it is more blessed to give than to receive.[59]

54 Eph 5:21
55 1 Cor 16:15-16
56 Ps 84:11
57 Ps 16:11
58 1 Tim 6:17
59 Acts 20:35

The character of the blessed One is that of giving. To give and to share mean to enlarge the benefit as well as to increase the joy of relationship.

The wisdom of God

God is of infinite wisdom. Wisdom may be defined as knowledge applied in purposeful activity to achieve good ends. Knowledge applied purposefully but not towards the good of others is not called wisdom but cunning. Wisdom must always be good. Wickedness is incompatible with wisdom.[60] God is of infinite power, infinite goodness and infinite knowledge. God's knowledge differs from ours in that it is prior to the existence of the things known. They exist because he knows them. Human knowledge is derived from observation and arises from experience. God does not have to wait on the event to know it as we do; he knows it before it happens and it only happens because he knows it and wills it.

It may be asked, 'How can knowledge be infinite, if knowledge has an object, for objects are limited?' It is because God knows possibilities as well as actualities. Thus God's knowledge is co-extensive with reality—not only actual reality, but all possible reality, which is infinite, so that he is of infinite knowledge. He knows all the actuality of reality as well as the infinity of its possibilities. This means that he knows how human wills will react to the circumstances in which they find themselves and which he himself controls. Therefore nothing takes God by surprise. He knows the end

60 Prov 8:7-8

from the beginning.[61] His infinite knowledge coupled with his infinite power and infinite goodness mean that he has infinite wisdom. Consequently, he infallibly achieves his purposes and those purposes are beneficent. He is active in forwarding the true interests of his whole creation.

God's wisdom is marvelously displayed in the created world. As the psalmist exclaims, "O Yahweh, how many are your works! In wisdom you have made them all."[62] The world has been created to accomplish ends of blessing, of joy and of fellowship with God. It marvellously achieves these ends. Take for example our body, that aspect of creation about which we know most. It has plainly been created in order that we might enjoy life. Our five senses all are vehicles of pleasure, as we see the beauty of the world, as we hear the sounds of music, as we taste the food which we need to sustain our life, as we enjoy the fragrance of a flower, as our bodies feel the sensation of the surf or of the wind. All these things are aspects of God's wisdom in conferring on us joys. Looked at from another point of view, the body is marvellously contrived to accomplish its ends of relationship, with all the pleasure—physical, mental, emotional, spiritual—that relationship brings. The eye, the face, the language structure of our brain, are designed to express our inner being to one another. Our sexual natures, both psychological and physical, are marvellously designed to relate us in joyous fellowship.

God's wisdom is manifest in creation but is even more marvellously displayed in redemption and the restoration

61 Isa 46:9-10
62 Ps 104:24

of fellowship with God. God has indeed bestowed upon us every spiritual blessing. These blessings are in Jesus Christ. He is the wisdom of God. He is so described by Paul in 1 Corinthians 1:24. God's beneficence comes to fruition in Christ and in his cross. Paul expresses this in Colossians 2:3—"Christ, in whom are all the treasures of wisdom… hidden".

Jesus described himself as the wisdom of God. In Luke 11:49 we read, "The wisdom of God [said], 'I will send to them prophets and apostles'". Comparison of this passage with its parallel in Matthew 23:34 shows that Jesus was speaking of himself.

A further example of our Lord's self-identification as the wisdom of God is in Matthew 11:19 and its parallel in Luke 7:35. In these passages, Jesus described the attitude of his generation who were rejecting the counsel of God. He compared them to children in the market-place. John the Baptist had called to them and they had taken no notice. Now Jesus called to them and they again took no notice. In Proverbs, wisdom calls in the marketplace to the passers-by, but her call is disregarded. "I have called and you refused. I have stretched out my hand and no man regarded; you have set at nought my counsel."[63] Luke 7:30 states explicitly, "The Pharisees and the lawyers rejected for themselves the counsel of God", and Jesus commented, "Wisdom is justified of all her children". In Matthew the same sentiment is put in different words: "Wisdom is justified by its works".[64] Jesus, the Wisdom of God, saw that his ministry was rejected by the

63 Prov 1:20ff., 8:1, 9:3
64 Matt 11:19

Jews, but nevertheless it is justified by what it accomplishes in those who are the children of wisdom.

Our Lord's knowledge that he was the wisdom of God spoken of in the Old Testament may be behind the somewhat unusual activity of public proclamation by Jesus when on the last great day of the feast he stood and cried, "If any man thirst, let him come to me, and drink". "This spoke he of the Spirit", says the evangelist.[65] Proverbs 1:21-23 reads, "[Wisdom] cries in the concourse... 'I will pour out my spirit upon you'", and in Proverbs 9:5 wisdom invites the passer-by, "Come, eat of my bread, and drink of my wine", a phrase that may have been in our Lord's mind also when he chose bread and wine to be symbols of his death, for the cross of Christ is pre-eminently the wisdom of God.[66]

Through the death of Jesus on the cross, God's wisdom is working out God's purposes—wisdom not guessed at for a moment by the rulers of this world, otherwise they would not have crucified the Lord of glory.[67] God's object, which he achieved through the death of Christ, was to overthrow evil, the great marring alien element in his creation, and to release those who are bound and blinded by Satan. This Christ accomplished by his death. So the cross is the wisdom of God. God accomplishes his ends through it. To the Jews it was a scandal, to the Greeks foolishness, but to those who were called, both Jews and Greeks, Christ the power of God and the wisdom of God.[68]

Christ as the wisdom of God is displayed not only in the

65 John 7:37-39
66 See 1 Corinthians 1:18-2:6.
67 1 Cor 2:7-8
68 1 Cor 1:23-24

cross, where most unexpectedly the very success of the evil powers in bringing Christ to destruction involved them in their own defeat, through the perfection with which Jesus bore all that evil which they brought upon him,[69] but is also seen in the way that the salvation of Christ is administered.

The whole work of our salvation is the wisdom of God. In 1 Corinthians 1, Paul pointed out that the way people are chosen is all part of God's wisdom. At first sight it would not appear the way of wisdom, for God chose the foolish in the world, God chose the weak, God chose the base things of the world and the things that are despised, in order that he might display his power and his grace in overthrowing and bringing to shame those who are boasting in their own strength apart from God.[70]

In Romans 11, Paul returned to the theme of God's wisdom as displayed in his predestinating purposes in carrying out the scheme of salvation and bringing the benefit of Christ's death to the world. In Romans 9, Paul reviewed the surprising turn of events where the people of God reject the provision of God for their salvation. In chapter 11, he drew out the consequences—that through this unexpected rejection by God's people of God's Word, the Gentiles have been brought into that blessing which in due course will embrace the Jews themselves, as a result of the very rejection of the gospel which had opened up the way for the conversion of the Gentiles. The apostle exclaimed, "Oh, the depths of the riches both of the wisdom and knowledge of God! How unsearchable are his judgements and unfathomable his

69 1 Cor 2:6-9
70 1 Cor 1:26-31

ways!"[71] And again, "God has shut up all unto disobedience that he might have mercy upon all".[72] The infinite wisdom of God is completing his purposes of blessing and salvation.

71 Rom 11:33
72 Rom 11:32

chapter 3

God in Trinity

The doctrine of the Trinity is the foundation of the Christian religion. Unless this doctrine is held firmly and truly, it is not possible to be a Christian. For the Christian is one who acknowledges Jesus as Lord, yet adheres to the religion of the Bible which emphasises so strongly that there is only one God.

The Christian message is "Believe in the Lord Jesus, and you shall be saved, you and your household".[1] Yet Jesus of Nazareth was a man who himself prayed to the Lord. Jesus was a man, yet his disciple Thomas acknowledged him as his Lord and his God, without thereby abandoning any tenet of his ancestral faith.[2] A knowledge of the doctrine of the Trinity resolves this conundrum and enables the Christian to believe in the Lord Jesus and in the God of the Bible.

The classical statement of the doctrine of the Trinity is the Athanasian Creed. Although it is fashionable today to denigrate the strong asseverations of the Athanasian Creed, and indeed this creed has been dropped by certain parts of Christendom, the statements of the creed remain true, in particular its opening statement: "Whosoever will be saved, before all things it is necessary that he holds the catholic faith. Which faith except everyone do keep whole and undefiled, without doubt he shall perish everlastingly. And

1 Acts 16:31
2 John 20:27-29

the catholic faith is this that we worship one God in Trinity and Trinity in unity, neither confounding the Persons nor dividing the Substance". The Athanasian Creed may be old fashioned in its language, but it is succinct and correct. Its strong words, that it is not possible to be saved without believing in the Trinity or in the reality of the incarnation, only spell out the gospel message that salvation is found only in Jesus the Lord. For Jesus cannot be called Lord apart from the doctrine of the Trinity.

A doctrine of revelation

The doctrine of the Trinity is derived entirely from the pages of the Bible. Its basis is the doctrine of the unity of God. God in his Word has revealed that he is God alone. There is but one living and true God. There is no other God. Monotheism is a doctrine of revelation. It is not a truth arrived at by human reflection. Ethnic religions are polytheistic. The three monotheistic religions, Judaism, Islam and Christianity, derive their faith in the unity of God from the Bible. The knowledge that there is but one God comes to us from God himself. He who speaks to us declares that he is the only divine being. All others are phantoms. This is the starting point. God reveals that he alone is God. God is one.[3] It is a truth which once known satisfies human thought. The human mind is monistic, and seeks to find a unity in experience. The doctrine of the unity of God, though not arrived at by human thought, confirms this human aspiration.

The doctrine of the Trinity waited for its full revelation

3 Deut 6:4

with the unfolding of the experience of salvation in Jesus Christ, and it depends on the authenticity of the revelation in Scripture. The Trinity is not a concept that the human mind can arrive at from its own resources. It is a historical fact that this doctrine has never occurred to anyone in any of the religions of the world outside the Christian revelation. Nor is it a doctrine that commends itself to the secular mind. At best it appears to be incomprehensible; more frequently it is scoffed at as absurd. Nevertheless, the doctrine is the glory of the Christian religion. Through it we understand not only God's nature and his relationship to us, but our own nature and our relationships to one another.

The doctrine of the Trinity is entirely drawn from the revelation of Holy Scripture and depends on the authority of Scripture. If the Christian view of the infallibility of Scripture, as taught by our Lord and his apostles and held uniformly throughout the Christian church up until a century or so ago, is abandoned, then the doctrine of the Trinity cannot stand. A great deal of modern theological writing is a tragic illustration of this fact. Once belief in the full inspiration, infallibility, reliability and trustworthiness of the whole of Scripture as the written Word of God is modified, then the doctrine of the Trinity is quickly lost. Knowledge of the trinitarian nature of God is only attained and understood if every word of Scripture is accepted as given by God's Spirit so that every word is given its full place in revelation. Scripture must be interpreted in accordance with Scripture, for the Spirit of God is uniform in his revelation. All Scripture is God-breathed and profitable for doctrine.[4] Apart from Scripture there is no ground for believing that God is Trinity and then in turn it becomes impossible to believe in the lordship of Christ without falling into polytheism.

The Trinity reveals that reality involves relationship

The doctrine of the Trinity is the glory of the Christian religion. It tells us that ultimate reality is personal relationship. God is ultimate reality, and is the ground of all other reality, and yet God is not a single monad or an impersonal absolute, but God is relationship. God is Trinity. He is not the unconscious, unmoved mover of Aristotle; nor is he the ground of our being, the one who lets be, of modern theology; but he is Father, Son and Holy Spirit. That God is a living God becomes plain when he addresses us. That he is a God of infinite goodness becomes plain not only from the content of his Word to us, but also from our confirmation of that goodness through our reflection of our own experience in the world.

Through the revelation of the Trinity we learn that the living God, the good and true God, is a God who has relationship within himself, and that the values of relationships ultimately belong to reality in its most absolute form. In the light of this doctrine, personal relationships are seen to be ultimate, are seen to be the most real things that are. The characteristic of true relationship is other-person-centredness. God is good, God is personal, God has relationship within himself, and because God is good these

4 2 Tim 3:16

relationships within the Trinity have the characteristic of other-person-centredness. Thus the Scriptures reveal that the Father loves the Son, and gives all things to the Son,[5] and that he shows him all that he does.[6] The Son in response does always that which pleases the Father.[7] His obedience springs from his love: "I love the Father, and as the Father gave me commandment, even so I do".[8] There is complete other-person-centredness in this relationship of the Father to the Son and of the Son to the Father. The Son does nothing of himself, but as the Father taught him.[9] The same is true of the relationship of the Spirit to the Father and the Son. The Spirit is self-effacing. He does not speak from himself, but he takes the things of the Son and shows them to believers; he glorifies Christ.[10] Ultimate reality is good, personal, relational. And these relationships are other-person-centred, as all good true relationships must be. This is the character of God and this is how creation has been made. We have been created in God's image for relationship, and this relationship must be other-person-centred.

The doctrine of the Trinity contradicts modern philosophical and social concepts. The idea of self-expression as the primary objective of life is very popular nowadays. Even in Christian circles we are being told that the first thing is to love ourselves. But these modern ideas are in contradiction to reality, to God in Trinity.

Similarly, the humanist ideal of the balanced complete

5 John 3:35
6 John 5:20
7 John 8:29
8 John 14:31
9 John 8:28
10 John 16:13-14

life as the object of living is again contrary to what is actual, for humanism is self-centred in ultimate analysis. God is Trinity; Trinity is relational. The relationships are good and personal and other-person-centred. The famous slogan of the French Revolution, which was the fruit of the Enlightenment, namely, 'Liberty, Equality, Fraternity', is in fact a denial of genuine relationship. Bestsellers today reflect the modern ideal of expressing yourself, of loving yourself, of liberating yourself from your relationships with other people, which constrict the development of your own personality. Through the revelation of the Trinity believers can see that this popular philosophical concept and social objective is contrary to reality and therefore will not bring the hoped-for benefits of happiness or peace. A renewal of understanding of the Trinity and its implications for the way human life should be based will lead to the recognition that personal relationships which are other-person-centred are ultimate in value for living, even though it should turn out that in serving these relationships it becomes impossible to pursue the chimera of gracious living, the balanced life and so-called authentic existence. Even life itself may be lost, but eternity will vindicate the reality of the basis of such actions. The modern philosophy of life known as existentialism concentrates on self-expression, 'living an authentic life', and this is translated into everyday language by the phrases 'doing your own thing', or 'doing what you like'. This is a very popular way of understanding true living today. People feel that they must express themselves, that they cannot be trammelled by their relationships with other people, whether with husband or wife or with children. They must be independent and pursue their own goals. This is not the way in which the Trinity relates. Eastern religions popular in the Western world today have the same concept of reality. Their followers are invited to 'meditate on yourself, worship yourself, repeat the mantra going on within you; God dwells within you as you'.

The doctrine of the Trinity contradicts and corrects these modern thoughts and attitudes. It teaches that reality seeks the welfare of the other person. Reality is good, it does not serve itself but serves others. And since this is ultimate reality, any philosophy of life or any social theory which contradicts this reality will certainly be running into the shallows.

Undivided but distinct

The relationship within the Trinity is very close. Jesus said, "I am in the Father and the Father in me",[11] and on another occasion, "The Father is in me and I am in the Father".[12] It is impossible to find a form of words which expresses a closer relationship. The words, "I am in the Father and the Father in me", maintain the distinction of the Persons, yet unite them so closely with one another that they are, as it were, identified with one another in their distinctness. The Father dwells in the Son and does the works that the Son does, and at the same time the Son dwells in the bosom of the Father and does everything that the Father shows him. The Father is in the Son, the Son is in the Father—a close intimate relationship. The same is true of the relationship of the Spirit to the Father and the Son.

11 John 14:10
12 John 10:38

This close unity of relationship within the Trinity is expressed in the theological dictum that in all God's works in the world, the Trinity is not divided. This truth reflects the language of Scripture. Thus in the supreme work of God in the world, the redemption of his people, scriptural language makes clear that the Trinity is not divided. Jesus bore our sins in his own body on the tree,[13] yet God was in Christ on the cross reconciling the world to himself,[14] and on the cross Jesus offered to the Father, through the eternal Spirit, the perfect sacrifice.[15] Though there is specific order in God's work in the world, yet this does not exclude the truth that the works of God in the world may be ascribed to any of the Persons of the Trinity. This is exemplified by our Lord's language when he promised his disciples divine assistance when they are brought to trial for their Christian faith. In Matthew 10:20 Jesus said, "It is not you who speak, but it is the Spirit of your Father who speaks in you". In Mark 13:11 he said, "It is not you who speak, but it is the Holy Spirit", and in Luke 21:15, "I will give you utterance".[16] Thus Father, Son and Spirit each receive the emphasis with regard to the same work of grace in the Christian. Similarly, in the works of Jesus' ministry, it was Jesus who was casting out devils. Yet he cast out devils by the Spirit of God, as he himself told his interrogators.[17] And yet it was the Father who was doing the works. Jesus was doing nothing of himself, but only what the Father taught him.[18] The Father who dwelt in

13 1 Pet 2:24
14 2 Cor 5:19
15 Heb 9:14
16 Literally, "I will give you a mouth".
17 Matt 12:28
18 John 8:28

him did the works: "The words which I say to you I do not speak on my own initiative, but the Father abiding in me does his works".[19] Father, Son and Spirit are one God. God is not divided in the works that he does in the world.

The unity of God is the basic concept underlying the revelation of the Trinity. The Persons of the Trinity are very closely related, yet they remain distinct but not separable. This close relationship is expressed by Jesus in the words "I am in the Father and the Father in me".[20] Jesus' relationship with the Spirit, and the Father's relationship with the Spirit, are expressed by the Spirit being named the Spirit of Jesus[21] and in another place the Spirit of the Father.[22] That is why the addition to the creed of the words "and from the Son", with regard to the relationship of the Spirit to the Father, is true and, although it was a late addition, it ought not to be removed simply to satisfy antiquarian interests or from a false ecumenism.

The first Christians were Jews who had come to acknowledge that Jesus of Nazareth was the Messiah promised by God to the Jewish people. In becoming Christians they did not change their religion. They continued to regard the Bible, that is, the Old Testament, as the oracles of God, believing, as Jesus taught them, that God spoke to them as they read. One of the most fundamental truths constantly reiterated and underlined in the Old Testament is that God is one. How did it come about that those who held the truth of the unity of God so firmly also came to believe in the

19 John 14:10
20 John 14:10
21 Acts 16:7; Phil 1:19
22 John 15:26; Rom 8:9-11

doctrine of the Trinity? It was the result of their experience of the facts. They could never give up the truth that God is one. That is so clearly taught in God's Word and written into the experience of the Jewish people. Yet they realized that Jesus was God. They applied Old Testament passages which speak of Yahweh directly to Jesus. There are many examples of this. One is the passage which begins with Paul's description of how "the Lord Jesus shall be revealed from heaven with his mighty angels in flaming fire, dealing out retribution to those who know not God".[23] Almost the whole of this passage is composed of quotations from Old Testament prophecies of which Yahweh is the subject.

From the beginning, Christians prayed to Jesus. Christians are described by Paul as those who "call upon the name of our Lord Jesus Christ" (that is, pray to Jesus).[24] Stephen is an example from the early chapters of Acts. He prayed as he died, "Lord Jesus, receive my spirit".[25] Christians recognized Jesus as their God. As Thomas put it when he first met the risen Christ, "My Lord and my God".[26]

It would have been easy for those brought up in the Greek culture to acknowledge many gods and many lords, but this was impossible for those brought up within the context of the revelation of God given to his people. To them, as Paul emphasised, there is only one God, and only one Lord.[27] But Jesus was God, and yet Jesus was not the Father; he himself prayed to his Father and described the Father as his God.[28]

23 2 Thess 1:7ff.
24 1 Cor 1:2
25 Acts 7:59
26 John 20:28
27 1 Cor 8:5-6
28 John 20:17

So the facts were simple, although perhaps difficult to comprehend. The Father was God and Jesus was God, and Jesus was not the Father and yet God was one. Fortunately in the Greek language there is a synonym for God, namely, Lord. This term had been used in the Greek translation of the Old Testament to translate the divine name 'YHWH', Lord of hosts. Paul makes use of this synonym in saying that for Christians there is one God the Father and one Lord Jesus Christ. God and Lord are synonyms, and yet the Father and Jesus are distinct. We have here the basis of the doctrine of the Trinity, which arose from the Christian experience of God in Jesus Christ and which was taught indeed by Christ himself. The revelation of the doctrine of the Trinity waited on the unfolding of the events of redemption, namely the incarnation of the Son and the pouring out of the Spirit.

New Testament doctrine

The character of God is other-person-centred, and thus Jesus in his earthly ministry was not given to drawing attention to himself. He did not bear witness of himself, and therefore his affirmation of his deity was not direct so much as indirect. It was very clear, nevertheless, and his followers came to a firm and clear conviction, based on our Lord's actions and teaching, that Jesus was divine, their Lord and their God. The miracles of Jesus testified not only to his messiahship, as when he reminded John the Baptist how Isaiah's prophecy of the Messiah was being fulfilled—the blind were seeing and the poor had the gospel preached to them[29]—but his miracles also pointed to his deity. In Psalm 107, it is God Almighty who

29 Matt 11:1-6

makes the storm to cease, the waves to be still, and brings the mariners to the haven where they wish to be. This our Lord did for his disciples on two occasions. He calmed the storm, the winds ceased, the waves subsided and they found themselves at the land where they were going. Again in the psalms, the people of Israel are depicted as complaining on their journey from Egypt to the promised land that they were left by God to starve in the desert, and they asked the question, "Can God prepare a table in the wilderness?"[30] God did so, sending them quails and manna. In the New Testament, the disciples of Jesus asked, "Where would we get so many loaves in a desert place to satisfy such a great multitude?",[31] but Jesus fed them, breaking and distributing the bread and the fishes. He provided a table in the desert.

It is, however, in John's Gospel, in the discourse in the upper room at the end of his ministry, that Jesus made quite clear to his disciples his equality with the Father and the intimate relationship between Father and Son. He told them that in as much as they had seen him, they had seen the Father. "He who has seen me has seen the Father" and "I am in the Father and the Father is in me".[32] John 17 is perhaps the most trinitarian chapter in the Bible. Absolute equality between the Father and the Son in the divine attributes is clearly enunciated. Although the Spirit is not mentioned specifically in this chapter, the Spirit is implied in the glory which Christ had given to his disciples, and which he himself had received from the Father. He is also the One

30 Ps 78:19
31 Matt 15:33
32 John 14:7, 9-10

who unites the disciples into one, and through whom Jesus indwells the disciples and the Father. So, too, in the last verse of the chapter, the Spirit is implied in the love with which the Father loved the Son, and which is in the disciples and which is equivalent to Jesus being in them. The Spirit is also implied in the unity arising from the mutuality of indwelling of the Father and Son and of believers with the Father and the Son.[33]

Everything that Jesus had, he had because it was given to him by the Father; this extends to his divine glory as well as to his human mission—note the constant repetition of "you gave me" in John 17, and also the statement "All yours are mine".

The Father is related to the Son, and the Son to the Father, through the Holy Spirit, as we are related to God through the Spirit: "As you, Father, are in me, and I in you, that they also may be in us".[34] The Spirit is love. "You loved me before the foundation of the world"[35] refers to an eternal relationship within the Trinity—before the foundation of the world. The Spirit is the glory, that is, the manifestation of the character of God. Christ prays for his return to the previous relationship of glory which he had with the Father from eternity: "Glorify me together with yourself, Father, with the glory which I had with you before the world was".[36] Christ has given us this same relationship of glory through the gift of the Spirit. It is a relationship one with another, similar to the relationship of the Father and the Son. The glory is the bond of unity

33 John 17:21
34 John 17:21
35 John 17:24
36 John 17:5

between ourselves, one with another, as well as between ourselves and God. "The glory which you have given me I have given to them; that they may be one, just as we are one, I in them and you in me..."[37] The Spirit is the glory, for the Spirit is the bond. Christ's prayer for unity of his followers with one another and with God was fulfilled at Pentecost with the gift of the Spirit. The Spirit is the oneness. The Spirit is the glory. The Spirit is love. The Spirit is the bond between Father and Son and between God and the believer, for the Spirit is the glory and the love. The Spirit's presence is the presence of Christ and the presence of love. Christ prayed, "The love wherewith you loved me may be in them, and I in them".[38] It is a grave theological mistake to think that our Lord's prayer for the unity of Christians is still to be fulfilled. It was answered at Pentecost.

The clearest teaching of the doctrine of the Trinity is given by our Lord in his final words to his disciples as recorded in Matthew 28:19. He sent them to baptize the nations into the knowledge of God and he puts it this way: "Baptizing them in the name of the Father and the Son and the Holy Spirit, teaching them to observe all that I commanded you". "The name of the Lord" was a frequent Old Testament phrase, which the disciples would be familiar with from their earliest youth.[39] Jesus took this phrase and expanded it. No longer is it the name of the Lord, that is, the name of Yahweh or Jehovah, but the name of the Father, Son and Holy Spirit. The unity of God is preserved by the singleness

37 John 17:22-23a
38 John 17:26
39 Gen 4:26, 12:8; Exod 33:19; Ps 102:15, 21; and some 80 other references.

of the name, and the Trinity of the Persons by the expansion of the term "the Lord" into Father, Son and Holy Spirit. God is three Persons, equal yet distinct. This verse has been rejected without grounds by some as a composition of the evangelist, but it is actually inconceivable that the Christian church did not have the doctrine of the Trinity from its earliest days, because from its foundation it regarded Jesus as God and prayed to Jesus as God, and yet maintained the distinction between Jesus and the Father, and the unity of the Father and the Son in the unity of God. At the same time it believed in the deity of the Spirit, whom Peter, for example, identified with God in his rebuke of Ananias.[40] The Spirit is the Spirit of God, yet is personal, for his actions are personal. He guides,[41] he grieves,[42] he intercedes.[43] He is a divine Person along with the Father and the Son. Even if Matthew had not recorded that Jesus had clearly taught his disciples the doctrine of the Trinity before his ascension, we should be compelled to conjecture that he had done so, in order to explain the worship of the first Christians.

It is a mistake to think that the New Testament church grew in its doctrine of the Trinity. The Christian church certainly grew in its ability to articulate the doctrine and to preserve the doctrine from the errors of heresy, but it held the doctrine from its earliest days, because of its experience of redemption in Christ and of the presence of Christ and the Father through the Spirit. These things were factual experiences of the early church and they

40 Acts 5:3-4
41 Rom 8:14
42 Eph 4:30
43 Rom 8:26

were put into their theological perspective by our Lord's teaching of the doctrine of the Trinity in the words of the great commission. Through these words the unity of God, so clearly taught in Scripture, is maintained; and the distinction, personality and equality of the persons within the Godhead are understood so that the three Persons in the one God may each be honoured and worshipped.

The New Testament is trinitarian to the core. God is praised in the Persons of the Trinity—Father, Son and Holy Spirit. Perhaps the most outstanding example of this is the opening chapter of Paul's letter to the Ephesians, which is trinitarian in structure. God the Father, God the Son and God the Holy Spirit are each in turn related to our redemption, to the praise of the glory of God's grace: "Blessed be the God and Father... who... fore-ordained us... to the praise of the glory of his grace... the Beloved, in whom we have our redemption through his blood... to the praise of [God's] glory; ...you were sealed with the Holy Spirit... to the praise of his glory".[44]

Old Testament doctrine

The doctrine of the Trinity is a doctrine of the New Testament. It is not revealed in the Old Testament, and cannot be gathered from the Old Testament alone. Yet it is present there, and this is not surprising, because the God of the Old Testament is the God of Trinity, and his Word in the Old Testament from time to time reflects this truth. Thus in the opening words of the Bible, "In the beginning, God created", the word for God is in the plural, literally "Gods",

44 Eph 1:3-14

but the verb "created", governed by this plural subject, is in the singular. Thus in the first verse of Scripture we have an indication of plurality, yet unity in the Godhead. In the same chapter we read, "And God said, 'Let us make man in our image'".[45] Whom is God addressing when he uses the plural "us"? Why is the plural "Let us make man in our image" followed immediately in the next verse by the singular, "God made man in *his* own image"? The phraseology is easily understood when it is remembered that the one true God here speaking is triune, three Persons in the relationship of unity. It is especially appropriate that this plurality of Persons in the Godhead should come to the surface in the Word of God at this point. For God is making man in his own image. Man is a relational person just as God himself is relational and the verse very neatly draws attention to this fact. It runs, "*In the image of God* created he *him*: male and female created he *them*".[46]

There are other interesting variations of language in the Old Testament which are intimations of the Trinity. In Genesis 32:24, it is said that Jacob wrestled with a man, yet Jacob commented, "I have seen God face to face".[47] Hosea said that Jacob had power with God and in the next verse that he had power over the angel.[48] In Exodus 23:20, the Lord said, "I will send an angel before you" and in the next verse "My name is in him". The one sent by Yahweh is Yahweh himself. In Malachi 3:1, we read, "The Lord whom you seek shall come suddenly to his temple, even the messenger of

45 Gen 1:26
46 Gen 1:27
47 Gen 32:30
48 Hos 12:3-4

the covenant whom you delight in, behold he comes, says Yahweh of hosts". The temple, of course, is God's temple, so that the messenger of the covenant, the hoped-for Messiah who is distinguished from Yahweh of hosts, is himself divine—a prophecy fulfilled by the coming of Christ. In Isaiah 48:16, a threefold distinction within the Godhead is reflected in the words of God: "From the time that it took place, I was there. And now the Lord Yahweh has sent me, and his Spirit." In this verse, there is a threefold distinction. The sent One is God, and yet he is sent by the Lord Yahweh with the Spirit of God.

But the clearest indication in the Old Testament that there is plurality in the Godhead is in the prediction that the Messiah whom God sends will be divine, as in the famous verse Isaiah 9:6: "For a child will be born to us, a son will be given to us; and the government will rest on his shoulders; and his name will be called Wonderful Counsellor, Mighty God, Eternal Father, Prince of Peace". This is an unambiguous prophecy that the Messiah will be divine. He will be both man and God: "a child will be born to us, a son will be given to us", yet this young child is also given the name "Mighty God, Everlasting Father", a prophecy which was fulfilled in Jesus, both God and man. The prophet adds, "The zeal of Yahweh of hosts shall perform this". Yahweh of hosts is the Sender. But the sent One, the child to be born, is also divine—Mighty God, Everlasting Father.

We see, then, that the doctrine of the Trinity is simply the fuller statement of the truth that God is one, and a consequence of the revelation of himself in Jesus Christ and of the gift of the Spirit in the redemptive process. It waited on the completion of that process for its full revelation.

This doctrine comes to the Christian, not as a burden on the mind, as the non-Christian assumes, but as a help in understanding the facts of redemption and the Christian experience of God. The Christian knows God as Father, he knows God as Son, he knows God as Spirit; yet it is not three Gods whom he knows, but one. The doctrine of the Trinity is an aid to his understanding of his experience of salvation.

Persons

The doctrine of the Trinity also fits our experience of personality. God is the highest being that we can conceive, and personality is the highest mode of being known to, or conceivable by, us. We believe that God is personal, but personality cannot exist in a monad, that is, in complete singularity of being. Personality requires relationship. The attributes of God are personal attributes. Justice is a mode of relationship. It is impossible to be just and righteous and fair in absolute isolation. So, too, wisdom has no meaning or content if there is no relationship. And this is particularly true of love. Only persons love; only persons are able to be loved. Indeed we may define a person as one capable of loving and of being loved.

Since we do not believe that God began to be righteous, wise and loving at creation, but is eternally so, we must either posit an eternal creation, as does the pantheist (but which is denied by the Scriptures and by common observation), or we must affirm the doctrine of the Trinity—that God is eternally relational, that there are eternal Persons within the unity of God, who are related righteously and lovingly. Indeed the doctrine is required to give a basis to our understanding of values. Love, self-sacrifice, goodness, fairness, faithfulness, are pre-eminent in our scale of values. They are personal and relational values, but if they do not exist in ultimate reality they cannot themselves be ultimate. But we believe them to be such, which we may dare to say approaches a proof of the doctrine of the Trinity, that is, that ultimate reality is relational, personal and good.

God is Trinity. This is clear from revelation. We may not know the fullness of God's being, but it would be foolish to say that the concept of Trinity is incomprehensible. For nothing that God has revealed is incomprehensible to those to whom he reveals it.

The doctrine of the Trinity throws light on the age-old philosophical problem promulgated by Plato of the one and the many. How can both universals and particulars be real? From the Trinity we realize that the relationship of one and many, in which the reality of the unity and the distinctiveness and reality of the particular are both preserved, is part of ultimate reality itself.

The doctrine also sheds light on our understanding of human life. From it we realize that personal relationship is of the essence of reality, and we also learn something of the quality of that relationship. It is a relationship of other-person-centredness. The Father loves the Son and gives him everything.[49] The Son always does that which pleases the Father.[50] The Spirit takes of the things of the Son and shows them to us. He does not glorify himself.[51] We learn from the Trinity that relationship is of the essence

49 John 3:35
50 John 8:29
51 John 16:13-15

of reality and therefore of the essence of our own existence, and we also learn that the way this relationship should be expressed is by concern for others. When Jesus lived among us he summed up his own life by the phrase: "I am among you as the one who serves".[52] The Trinity in its relationship was manifested in human relationships where the man Christ Jesus served others as God serves us, and as within the Trinity itself there is concern by the Persons of the Trinity one for another.

The Word and the Spirit

From the doctrine of the Trinity we also see the appropriateness of the Son's becoming incarnate. He always does that which pleases the Father. He does nothing of himself, but only as he is taught of the Father.[53] He is in this way the expression of God, and therefore when God expresses himself in human life by becoming man yet remaining God, it is the Son whom the Father sends. It is the Son who becomes incarnate. The Father has given the Son everything.[54] It is the Son who serves mankind by giving his life.[55] The Son, or the Word of God, is the expression of God within the Trinity and therefore the expression of God towards us in the incarnation. It is the eternal Word that becomes flesh.[56] The Son is the One sent and he expresses among us the words and actions of the Father who is in him, and he in the Father.

52 Luke 22:27
53 John 8:28-29
54 John 3:34-35
55 Mark 10:45
56 John 1:1-14

The names of the Persons of the Trinity, as revealed in Holy Scripture, reflect the eternal relations of the Trinity as well as the work of the Trinity in the world. The Son is the Word of the Father. Our words are us. They are the expression of our minds, and our words are conveyed to others by our breath. Now the Spirit is the breath of God—'spirit' and 'breath' are identical both in Hebrew and Greek. It is by God's Spirit or breath that we are related to God through his Word. Breath is movement from God to us; we know God through his Word by means of his breath, by means of his Spirit. But breath in itself is nothing; it must carry words to be the means of relationship; so the Spirit of God does not testify of himself but takes of the things of Jesus, who is the Word and expression of God, and shows them to us.[57]

Secondly, breath is the sign of life. At the beginning of the world, in the gloom and chaos, the breath of God was present brooding over the waters.[58] The breath was the agent in bringing the world and its life into being, for God spoke, "Let there be light". He spoke his word through his breath, and the world, pulsating with life, came to be.

At the creation of man God breathed into man and he became a living soul,[59] and at the recreation of the sinner into the child of God, it is the breath or Spirit of God who brings life through the Word of God.

God, the Word of God, the breath or Spirit of God are divine and eternal and, as we learn from the New Testament, all are personal and distinct, yet one God.

57 John 16:13-15
58 Gen 1:2
59 Gen 2:7

Man, the image of God

The doctrine of the Trinity also enables us to understand what is meant when it is said that God created man in his own image. God has created us for relationship, for he is relational. We know that our nature is relational, for we do not like being isolated. Loneliness is horrid. The way the human race is structured shows clearly that we are created for relationships. Genesis 1:27 runs, "God created man in his own image. In the image of God created he him; male and female created he them." Men and women together make up the human race. Men and women complement each other and together make up humanity.

Theologians have puzzled over whether the Fall has meant the loss of the image of God or simply its marring. Both are true. Fallen man is still in the image of God according to Genesis 9, and yet he is very far from the image of God. That image has been restored in Christ, who is the image of God.[60] So from one point of view the image has been lost completely, but from another it is an inalienable part of human nature. It is not difficult to reconcile these two apparently irreconcilable concepts when we realize that the image of God means relationship. The Trinity is relationship, and humanity is relationship. So that when God created us in his own image, this has a double aspect. Firstly, he gave to us the basic faculties and characteristics on which relationships are based, and then on these he built the perfect flowering of that relationship in the first human pair. Adam and Eve were perfectly related to one another and perfectly related to God. The possibility of relationships

60 Col 1:15

is based on personal attributes, that is to say, on such things as reflective self-consciousness, and mind which is able to remember the past and plan for the future; on will, which is able to direct actions towards purpose; on a moral sense and consciousness, which assess actions in accordance with relationship; on a religious sense, from which we learn that we are dependent on a superior being; and on the faculty of language, through which one mind is able to relate to another. These characteristics, which enable humanity to be persons, have never been lost and that is why in Genesis 9 we are told we are not to raise our hand against our fellow man because he has been created in the image of God. Our fellow man is in relationship with God and with us as a person. That is why Genesis 9 forbids us to kill him though the same chapter gives permission for the killing of animals for food.

Yet personal relationships, although they are based on personal characteristics and gifts, do not flower into true relationships unless they are crowned with moral actions and attitudes such as love, kindness, faithfulness, service and consideration. It is these moral virtues that have been lost through the Fall, so completely that instead of the relationship being one of serving one another, as is the case within the Trinity, and as God serves us and as he intended that we should serve one another, this relationship has been completely marred. The moral gifts by which the relationship is perfected and expressed have been lost. Self-centredness has taken the place of service and devilish character has begun to supplant the character and image of God. However, in Christ that image has been restored in its entire and moral perfection. He was a human person relating to his fellow men through all the personal structures of our nature, but he also built on those structures the perfection of personal relationships in a way we never achieve. He was always in a personal relationship of perfect love, trust and obedience with his heavenly Father, and in a perfect personal relationship with his fellow men, loving them, forgiving them, having compassion on them and serving them. Jesus is the perfect image of God, being perfect Man, and as we come to him and dwell in his company we are transformed by his Spirit into the same image, reflecting more and more the glory, that is, the character and Spirit of God.[61]

The doctrine of the Trinity helps solve another problem which troubles modern theologians. How is it possible that human language drawn from human experience can be an adequate vehicle for describing the ineffable God? Must all language be merely analogical when it is used to describe the realities of religion? That is a very popular view. Religious language is thought to be analogical and not direct description, but if this were true it would mean we have no sure knowledge of God, for we cannot be sure how an analogy fits unless we already know the object which the analogy describes—that is, unless we already know God, we cannot know whether analogical language fits the God of whom we are speaking. In other words, this line of thought means that we have no sure knowledge of God and this is a conclusion of much modern theology.

However, the doctrine of the Trinity reminds us that human life has been created in the image of God. Human relationships reflect the image of the Trinity. It follows

61 2 Cor 3:18

that human language reflecting these human relationships is a suitable vehicle to describe God's relationships within himself and with humanity, for we have been created in his image and our relationships correspond to his relationships, for they are an image of them. It follows that when God chooses human language to describe his relationships, not only within himself but especially his relationships to us, he is not using analogical language but a direct description of reality, for the language being used is language drawn from the image of that reality. It is God who is using the language (for he is inspiring the prophet), and the vehicle that he is using (human language) is adequate, indeed exact, to describe what would otherwise be beyond our powers of knowing. Because we have been created in the image of God, the revelation of God to us becomes a possibility. We may know him truly through our own human language. Had this not been so, it would not be possible to have the Christian religion, which is a religion of faith, trust, obedience and love. For it is not possible to relate personally to one who is only known by analogy, to one about whom you are not sure and of whom you only have vague and general concepts. But God reveals himself to us personally in a direct and literal and not merely analogical way, and so we are able to respond in a real and true way and enter into real personal relationships with God. All this follows from the fact that God is Trinity and has created us in his image, that is to say, to be relational, so that the language which describes our relationships is an adequate vehicle when used by God himself to describe the real relationships that he has within himself and with us. In other words, religious language is not analogical but direct and univocal. We may rely on it. When God uses it to describe the relationship between himself and us it has the same meaning as when used to describe our relationships with one another, because human life has been created in the image of God who himself is relational.

Order

There is order in the Trinity: Father, Son, Spirit. This order does not imply inferiority but is an order among equals; yet it is not reversible, for irreversibility is of the essence of order. The very terms 'Father' and 'Son' indicate order, and it is of the essence of order that it cannot be disturbed or reversed without creating disorder and disharmony. From the doctrine of the Trinity, we learn that there is order in ultimate reality. God is a God of order. This suggests that there is also order in created life. If the order of relationships in created life is confused, the relationships will be jarred. Paul saw this very clearly in church life at Corinth. He said God was a God of order and therefore things should be done in proper order;[62] and he commended the Colossians for their order.[63] Order does not imply subservience or inequality. Father/Son indicates an order which is not reversible, but which is equal. The Father is greater than the Son, but not as we evaluate greatness; for according to the real values of God, the servant is the greatest; subordination is not an indication of inequality but of order. There cannot be subservience where there is complete love, complete other-person-centredness. In the Trinity, although there is order there is no dominance on the one hand or subservience on

62 1 Cor 14:31-40
63 Col 2:5

the other, but only a relationship of love.

The doctrine of the Trinity shows us that order is of the essence of reality, so it is to be expected that God has created the world with order. This is in fact plain if we look at the created world around us where we see the different species all ordered. Genesis 1 describes how God created order from chaos in six ordered stages. So, too, in the creation of humanity God has created order. Though men and women are equal they stand in an order of relationship. There is an order of headship and of response, an order which reflects the character of God as constituted in the Trinity. The world in general, and humanity in particular, have been created by God and all that fills the earth is a reflection of his character. Christian congregations and Christian homes should reflect this order, which is a reflection of the character of God himself. The outsider should be able to see God's character reflected in the way the congregation orders itself and Christian families should learn from the order of the congregation how their own homes should be conducted. The conduct of the congregation should not contradict the order that God has structured in the world and in human society, and in particular in married life, which has specially been created in the image of God, as Paul pointed out in Ephesians 5.

Paul made clear what this order in created humanity is when he said that the head of every man is Christ, the head of woman is the man and the head of Christ is God.[64] Some modern translations have obscured Paul's meaning by limiting his statement to married women. But the Greek shows that it is not so. And this modern translation is

64 1 Cor 11:3

objectionable, for it implies that on entering the divinely ordered state of matrimony a woman exchanges freedom for subservience. The problem in Paul's statement must not be resolved by restricting headship to marriage, but by understanding the true meaning of headship as exemplified by God's headship of Christ and Christ's headship of humanity. Headship implies order and the order of the congregation should acknowledge God's created order in humanity, and not turn it topsy-turvy or reverse it. This means that men (whether a group or individuals) must not dominate in the congregation, for the head of *every* man is Christ. The congregation will have leaders, to whom all should submit within their area of leadership, but the leadership must not be that of dominance or autocracy, for the head of every man is Christ, and Christ alone. This order must also be reflected in the relationships between men and women in the congregation. Headship implies responsibility and initiative in welfare, and if this is to be discharged properly all must acknowledge that God has created order in relationship in humanity, and it will be a help to see that this reflects the order eternally subsisting in the Trinity. If we destroy order in the congregation, we will destroy order in the Christian home and that will bring great sadness. We will also set an example which will destroy order in society. Our homes and our society, as well as our congregations, should reflect the order which is part of their constituent created nature and is an image of the order in the Trinity. The Son does not strive to be the Father or feel inferior because he is not the Father.

From the relationship of the Trinity we understand what headship means. There is no hint of dominance in it, simply initiative in service. This and this only is the headship that God has conferred on men in respect to women. So, too, from the relationship within the Trinity we learn what the response of obedience is. There is no hint of subservience in it, only the glad and grateful response to the initiatory service and care of the head. Sin has debased headship into dominance and obedience into servility. This is the way the Gentiles behave.[65] But it is not to be so among Christians, for God has given the grace of his Spirit to enable them to live and to relate to one another in the way he intended when he created men and women in his image.

There is equality yet order among the Persons of the Trinity. This is the key for human relationships in the congregation, in the home and in society. Yet equality in the Trinity is not sameness, nor does it mean the disregard of what is implicit in order. Jesus said, "I and the Father are one"[66] and "All that is mine is yours and yours mine".[67] But he also said, "The Father is greater than I".[68] It is possible so to stress equality, for example, within the congregation, that disorder and lack of relationship emerge; or on the other hand, so to stress order that dominance emerges and destroys relationship. It is especially important that the congregation, which is the outward and visible sign of Christ's church and of the heavenly life, should reflect the principle of equality and order, which is basic to reality itself, so that the rest of society may learn from the way it sees Christians ordering their lives.

65 Mark 10:42-45
66 John 10:30
67 John 17:10
68 John 14:28

chapter 4

One Lord, Jesus Christ

The friends of Jesus believed that he was God. They were all devout Jews and if there was any truth that they believed from the bottom of their heart it was that there is only one God. Every morning they would say those words from Deuteronomy "Hear O Israel! Yahweh is your God, Yahweh is one".[1] Yet they believed that Jesus was God and worshipped him as God.

It is not a view that they came to suddenly, but it grew over the months and years that they knew him, so that at the end they were able to affirm with complete conviction and sincerity that Jesus was God. Thomas is recorded as ascribing deity to Jesus with the apostrophe, "My Lord and my God".[2] John begins his Gospel with the statement that the Word, that is, Jesus of Nazareth, was God. In Hebrews 1, the writer applied the Old Testament psalm to Jesus "Thy throne, O God, is for ever and ever".[3] Paul described Jesus as "God over all".[4] Though it is true that some modern English translations separate this ascription of deity from Christ, in doing this the translators are not following the text but their own theological presuppositions. Every grammatical and stylistic consideration makes clear that Jesus was the One to whom Paul was referring when he spoke of "God over

1 Deut 6:4
2 John 20:28
3 Heb 1:8
4 Rom 9:5

all, blessed for ever". In Titus 2:13, Paul very clearly spoke of Jesus as "our great God and Saviour" whose appearing we are all awaiting expectantly.

Jesus' friends did not hesitate to apply to Jesus passages from the Old Testament which refer to Yahweh. Thus Mark began his Gospel by saying that John the Baptist was the one who fulfilled the prophecy of Isaiah: "The voice of one crying in the wilderness, make ready the way of Yahweh, make his paths straight".[5] That prophecy is referred to John the Baptist's preparation for the ministry of Jesus. Jesus was Yahweh, whose way John the Baptist was making ready.

Not only the New Testament but also contemporary secular literature endorses the fact that the first Christians believed that Jesus was God. About 80 years after the crucifixion, Pliny, the Governor of Bithynia on the shores of the Black Sea, wrote a letter to the Roman emperor in which he described Christian worship and said that Christians in his area would come together early in the morning to sing hymns to Jesus as God. From the beginning of the Christian church, Christians prayed to Jesus. This is the way that Christians are defined by Paul in 1 Corinthians 1:2. They are people who call upon the name of the Lord. For a Jew or a believer in the Old Testament to pray to Jesus meant that he regarded Jesus as the one and only God.

The Old Testament prophets foretold that the Messiah, that is the Christ, would be God Almighty, their Lord, Yahweh. The most famous passage is Isaiah 9, "For a child will be born to us, a son will be given to us… and his name will be called… Mighty God, Everlasting

5 Mark 1:3; Isa 40:3

Father".[6] The Messiah is Emmanuel—God with us.[7] Isaiah's contemporary, Micah, predicted that the ruler in Israel who should come from Bethlehem should be one whose "goings forth are from long ago, from the days of eternity".[8] Ezekiel, in his prophecy of the good shepherd, brought into one the Lord Yahweh and the coming Messiah: "Thus says the Lord Yahweh, 'Behold, I myself will search for my sheep and seek them out… I will deliver them… I will bring them out from the peoples and gather them… I will feed them in a good pasture… I will feed my flock and I will lead them to rest', declares the Lord Yahweh. 'I will seek the lost, and bring back the scattered, bind up the broken and strengthen the sick'."[9] And in verse 23, God speaks, "My servant David… will feed them; he will feed them himself and be their shepherd". Thus Yahweh is the Good Shepherd and Yahweh's servant David is the Good Shepherd. Both are the one shepherd who feeds God's sheep. This prophecy of Ezekiel was applied by Jesus to himself.[10] He is the Good Shepherd who sought for his sheep, who brought the sheep out from the nations and gathered them into one fold, who protected them and provided for them, leading them out into good pasture and who in the end laid down his life for the sheep. He delivers them and none is able to pluck them out of his hand, and yet it is not he alone, but the Father in him, and none is able to pluck them out of the Father's hand.[11]

6 Isa 9:6
7 Isa 7:14; Matt 1:23
8 Mic 5:2
9 Ezek 34:11-16
10 John 10:1-18
11 John 10:28-29

Jesus' self-testimony

Jesus knew himself to be God. This became plain at the end of his ministry. He knew that he came forth from God and that he was going to God.[12] Jesus' knowledge of his deity is reflected in his question to the Pharisees about David's son and David's Lord.[13] It was an indirect affirmation, asking the Pharisees to reflect on what they had already received from the Old Testament. This indirectness is in keeping with the character of God. Jesus did not bear witness to himself, did not take the initiative in announcing his own person with clear and bold affirmations, but the truth of his person was reflected in his actions, in his miracles—for example, when he met the needs of his hearers by providing them with loaves and fishes through a miraculous divine creation.[14] Jesus' identification of himself with the wisdom of God is an affirmation of deity, for wisdom is inalienable from God. God's wisdom cannot be divorced from God himself. Moreover, it is the prerogative of God alone to send prophets to speak in the name of God. In the Old Testament God is characterized as one who sends prophets to his people.[15] Yet Jesus says, "I will send prophets",[16] and again "The wisdom of God says, 'I will send prophets'".[17] Christ is the wisdom of God and Christ is divine.

An interesting affirmation by Jesus of his deity, so indirect that it is hardly noticed, is the message that he told his disciples to give to the owners of the colt on which he

12 John 13:3
13 Matt 22:42-46
14 Mark 6:33-44
15 2 Chr 36:15; Jer 7:25
16 Matt 23:34
17 Luke 11:49

was to ride into Jerusalem.[18] When the owners asked the disciples what they were doing loosing the colt, they replied as Jesus had instructed them, "Its owner needs it".[19] The contrast between the human owners and Jesus is clear in the Greek. Thus at the end of his ministry, our Lord made it clear that he is the divine Owner of all things. He is the sovereign God the Creator. He is Lord of all.

From the beginning of his ministry, Jesus recognized his divine authority. His words were as true and as authoritative as were the Ten Commandments which had been spoken directly by God from heaven. "You have heard that the ancients were told, 'You shall not commit murder'... But I say to you..."[20] Jesus placed his words, spoken to the disciples from the mountain in Galilee, on the same level as the words spoken by God from Mount Sinai. For Jesus was the Lord Yahweh. Jesus was conscious that in himself God was present with his people. The Father was in him and he was in the Father.[21] He is the One whose name is "I am".[22]

Thus the whole of Scripture, Old Testament and New, Jesus himself, his apostles and the early Christians combine in testimony to the marvellous miracle that God dwelt with men in Jesus Christ. Not that there was any change in the Godhead, for God is unchangeable, but there was a change in God's relationship to creation. The Creator had come into

18 Luke 19:28-35
19 This is not reflected in most English versions. The Greek of Luke 19:33 reads, translated literally, "And as they were untying the colt, its masters (*kurioi*) said to them, 'Why are you untying the colt?' And they said, 'Because its master (*kurios*) has need'."
20 Matt 5:21-22
21 John 14:10-11
22 John 8:58

a new relationship with his creation by taking the nature of men, whom he had created to have dominion and to be in his image. For although Jesus was fully God and there is no doubt as to the Bible testimony to this truth, he was at the same time truly and fully man. None of his contemporaries doubted that. His physical life was human. From time to time he was tired[23] and hungry,[24] and his life terminated in pain on the cross. He died and was buried. His emotional life was human. He had friends;[25] he wept.[26] His religious life was human. He prayed and trusted God.[27] His knowledge was human. It grew and increased from babyhood onwards.[28] There were times when he was surprised at the way events turned out. There were things which he did not know. In taking our nature and becoming man, Jesus accepted all the limitations of perfect human nature. Thus he accepted the limitation of knowledge which goes with human life. For example, he did not know what was, humanly speaking, contingent either on other people's wills or on the events of nature. For example, he did not know who touched him in the crowd. This is plain from the way Luke described the incident.[29] Nor did he know that there were no figs on the fig tree when he made a detour to it in order to satisfy his hunger.[30] He did not know the moment of his arrest, as a careful reading of the synoptic accounts makes clear. And

23 Mark 4:38
24 Matt 21:18
25 John 15:14-15
26 John 11:35
27 Matt 26:39
28 Luke 2:52
29 Luke 8:43-48
30 Mark 11:12-13

Jesus himself told his disciples that he did not know the day or the hour of the inauguration of God's final kingdom.[31]

It is plain from the narrative that our Lord in his earthly life did not have the omniscience of God, and yet his knowledge was well beyond ours—not only his knowledge of the Father, but his knowledge of man. We read that he knew what was in man and did not need anyone to bear testimony to it.[32] He knew who it was who should betray him. Our Lord's knowledge was human knowledge, yet it was knowledge drawn from his close association and unity with the Father. That relationship was perfect and so his knowledge was perfect, though not complete. It was perfect because it was according to the will of God. Just as his words and works were not from himself, but he taught and did what the Father showed him, so, too, we may say that his knowledge was drawn from his relationship with the Father. There were some things which the Father retained in his own hands. These things our Saviour did not know in his incarnate life. What he knew he learnt from the Father, doubtless through what we would call natural means, though no doubt sometimes through direct revelation.

We do not know the process by which our Lord learnt, though some part of it at least would be the same as that by which we learn, that is, studying the Old Testament, observing how things happen, meditating and reflecting on all this and asking questions of those who knew more than he did. But in addition there would be that very close relationship with the Father which brings a deepening

31 Mark 13:32
32 John 2:24-25

understanding and knowledge, which humanity, cut off from God through rebellion, does not have, but which Christians, through their renewed relationship to God through the Spirit, begin to appreciate and understand. Had it not been for the Fall, our relationship with God would have continued perfect, growing daily in depth so that our knowledge would have been perfect, for we would have been taught of God, and have grown daily, and in this way humanity would have avoided all those natural evils and disasters which cause some to stumble in their faith in the God of infinite power and love.

Although our Lord's knowledge was limited, as all human knowledge is, yet his sinlessness, or in other words his perfect relationship with God, prevented him from saying anything which he knew to be beyond his knowledge. Therefore all his words are utterly reliable and none will pass away, as he himself affirmed.[33] Limitation in knowledge in no way implies error in knowledge.

Jesus, our complete example

Our Lord was truly human and perfectly human. Because of his perfect humanity and the divinity of his person, Jesus is the complete example of how human life should be lived, the values on which it should be based and the attitudes which should characterize it. For in Jesus, the Designer himself was living his product. God the Creator was living the life he intended to be lived. Though much could be said under this heading, one or two points will suffice, suitable for the present times.

33 Matt 24:35

The first is that Jesus set the example of a life free from materialism. He chose to live a simple life. He was brought up in the country village of Nazareth. During much of his ministry, he had no permanent dwelling-house,[34] and he inculcated, not only by example, but by direct teaching, the need for men and women to be freed from material-mindedness. He gave the command: "Do not be anxious for your life, as to what you shall eat, or what you shall drink; nor for your body, as to what you shall put on".[35] This command is perhaps the one which is most consistently and flagrantly disobeyed by Christians in our society. It is regarded simply as a piece of idealistic advice, but our Lord couched it in the form of a command. We are to seek God's kingdom, knowing that God will look after and provide for our needs.[36] Put more colloquially, if we look after the affairs of God, he will look after our affairs. But most of us put our own affairs on an equality with those of God. We seek to look after both together. It cannot be done, but if we wish to look after our own affairs God allows us to do this, yet we are in actual disobedience and therefore cannot expect to grow in spiritual depth. For it is a failure of faith. It shows that we do not believe the clear teaching of Jesus that God, who provides for the birds their daily food, will much more provide for us if we give our attention, our time and our activity to seeking and advancing his kingdom and his righteousness. Materialism may be disguised by our telling ourselves that we are really seeking the advantages

34 Matt 8:20
35 Matt 6:25
36 Matt 6:31-34

of our family when we seek for higher pay or better housing or more ample superannuation. But this is simply to deceive ourselves and to make the end justify the means.

Another example that our Lord has given is the example of service. Jesus summed up his life in the phrase, "I am among you as the one who serves".[37] In this, he was reflecting the character of God, whose tender mercies are over all his works[38] and who provides for our needs, for men and women as well as for the rest of creation.[39] The Christian's aim should be to serve those with whom he is brought into contact by the flux of events. God controls the events that enter our lives, and they are for the purpose of our exhibiting the character of Christ.[40]

In the managing of our money the same principle holds. We should serve those with whom we are brought into contact by our money. For example, property owners should serve their tenants. Christ in his human life set us the example that we are to serve, even though that service is costly as it was in his case. He told his disciples he came not to be served, but to serve to the extent of giving his life as a ransom for others.[41]

Perfect faith

The chief example that our Saviour has left us is the example of faith. He lived his life in perfect faith in God. Faith is a human activity. It is the response that we should make to

37 Luke 22:27
38 Ps 145:9
39 Psalm 104; see especially verses 27-28.
40 Eph 2:10
41 Mark 10:45

the faithfulness of God. God is faithful and he expresses his faithfulness in promises. We exercise faith towards that faithfulness of God by believing those promises and living our life in the light of them. This is how Jesus lived and so he has become the exemplar of faith. In Hebrews 11, there is a catalogue of the heroes of faith. Beginning with Abel, the list includes Enoch, Noah, Abraham, Jacob, Joseph, Moses, right through to David, Samuel and the prophets. But the chief of all is Jesus. He is the One to whom we are to look, for he is the Captain and Perfecter of faith, who for the joy that was set before him endured the cross.[42]

Faith is a human activity; it looks to the unseen;[43] it cannot be exercised in the sphere of omniscience. Faith is impossible if knowledge is complete. But human knowledge is limited, and this limitation of knowledge is the occasion for our exercising faith in the Word of God, who knows the future in a way that we do not.

The events leading up to the crucifixion are an example of how Jesus lived by faith. To go up to Jerusalem for the Passover was a religious obligation on every Jewish man. It was commanded in the law of God. But it was plain that for Jesus to go up to Jerusalem for the Passover was a very hazardous undertaking. Especially since the raising of Lazarus, the Jewish authorities had been seeking to arrest Jesus, and he had been staying away in the desert the other side of Jordan.[44] To go to Jerusalem was full of risk. His disciples warned him against it. They knew real danger to

42 Heb 12:2
43 Heb 11:1; cf. Rom 8:24-25
44 John 11:54; cf. 7:1, 10:40

life, not only for Jesus, but for themselves was impending at Jerusalem. Jesus did not shrink from his duty, yet he took every precaution. During the day, from early morning, he was teaching in the temple surrounded and so protected by the crowds. The upper room where he ate the Passover was only known to himself, and the two disciples who prepared it were directed there by what was apparently a prearranged sign between Jesus and the householder. Afterwards he retired to a secret place known only to his disciples. It was here that Judas, one of those who knew, turned traitor and revealed to the chief priests how they could arrest Jesus away from the crowds.

Jesus knew how things were turning out. In the Garden of Gethsemane he took the opportunity of the silent night to beseech his Father in prayer that events might be reversed, that the cup which was looming might pass away from him.[45] He set three of his disciples to watch while he prayed. He said to them, "My soul is deeply grieved to the point of death; remain here and keep watch".[46] Though he felt the need of prayer as never before, yet he took precautions. This was his duty, for it is never right to take unnecessary risks. The three disciples failed him and the Jewish and Roman soldiery, led by the disciple Judas, approached undetected. At the end of his time of prayer, he told his disciples that they might go on sleeping and take their rest, presumably because he would take over the duty of watchfulness.[47] Jesus, however, became aware that Judas' band was close at hand.

45 Mark 14:36
46 Mark 14:34
47 Mark 14:41

He reversed his concession to allow them to go on sleeping. "Stop", he said, "the crisis has arrived; I am betrayed; get up; let us go".[48] But it was too late. While he was still speaking, Judas burst through the darkness, came up to him and kissed him. It is interesting that all three synoptic Gospels emphasize the fact that while Jesus was still speaking, the denouement came. And both Matthew and Mark say that our Lord's last words were "Let us go", but it was too late.[49] The events showed Jesus that his prayer had been answered in a way that he had hoped it might not be. He saw the events that were overtaking him as the cup which his Father was giving him, and so he willingly drank it. He gave himself up in order that his disciples might escape.

Calvary

Jesus' faith never failed, even when it was tested to the limit on the cross. There, during those three hours of darkness, the Lord laid on him the iniquity of us all.[50] He was made sin.[51] He was cursed by God with the curse that every sinner deserves to experience. He became a curse for us, as Paul put it.[52] Yet through it all there was never a moment of recrimination; never a fist shaken, as it were, in the face of God; never a thought of self-pity. His thoughts and words were only for others: a word to secure the safety of his disciples at his arrest;[53] a look to secure the recovery of

48 Paraphrasing Mark 14:41-42.
49 Mark 14:42; Matt 26:46
50 Isa 53:6
51 2 Cor 5:21
52 Gal 3:13
53 John 18:8

Peter after his denial;[54] a prayer for the forgiveness of those who were crucifying him;[55] a word of comfort and promise of heavenly bliss to a fellow sufferer now repentant;[56] a word of provision for the dear one left desolate.[57] Towards his heavenly Father there was full faith. His love and trust of God never wavered, even when he was deserted by God (and deserted justly, for he was the sinbearer) and was experiencing the depths of what sin does for humanity. He was forsaken by God.[58] God gave the sinner up, as Paul put it in Romans 1.[59] Christ was identified with our sin. He who knew no sin was made sin for us.[60] He bore our sins in his own body on the tree.[61] He went down into the very depths of hell, symbolized by the darkness[62] and the cursed tree, but experienced in reality and expressed by the cry from the cross, yet in the extremity of this experience his love and faith in God never wavered. God was still his God, the one to whom he could pray and address his petition: "My God, my God, why have you forsaken me?"[63] He came out of that experience justified, and he died committing his soul into the hands of his heavenly Father: "Father, into your hands I commit my spirit".[64]

54 Luke 22:61
55 Luke 23:34
56 Luke 23:39-43
57 John 19:26-27
58 Mark 15:34
59 Rom 1:24, 26, 28
60 2 Cor 5:21
61 1 Pet 2:24
62 Matt 27:45
63 Mark 15:34
64 Luke 23:46

Obedience

Faith leads to obedience and faith expresses itself through obedience. The two are inseparable. Jesus' faith was perfect, and so his obedience was complete.[65] His faith was tested in a way that ours never will be. God asked of him a form of obedience which he never will ask of us. God asked that he, the perfect man, should identify himself so completely with sinful man that he became sin for us and experienced all that sin involves. His faith and obedience are an example to us that we also should trust and obey. In this sense, our faith and obedience are similar to our Lord's. They have the same formal character. We are to be perfectly obedient to God.[66] Nevertheless, the material content of how we are to obey is very different. For our part, we are to keep the law of God and follow the example of Christ of loving God with all our hearts, and loving and serving one another. Jesus also fulfilled all this and was fully obedient and perfect in all these human duties. His faith was tested throughout his life.

We are given a glimpse of this testing in the narration of the temptations at the beginning of our Lord's ministry.[67] There was no corner of human experience which was not explored by Satan to bring our Lord to disobedience. Finally, on the cross with all its cruelty and indignities, and in the depths of hell, Christ triumphed over Satan. On the cross, Jesus was asked by his heavenly Father to undergo an experience through which mankind has been saved;

65 Heb 5:8-9
66 Matt 5:48
67 Matt 4:1-11

namely, to undergo the experience of bearing our sins, bearing them perfectly and obediently without any failure of faith or of love. In this way Jesus achieved what humanity had never yet achieved—perfect obedience to God tested to the fullest extent imaginable. In him, the Father was always well pleased.[68] And because he has borne the pangs of hell obediently and lovingly, he has triumphed over all that Satan and evil are able to effect.[69] He was the Victor, and God vindicated him by raising him from the dead and exalting him to the throne, crowned with glory and honour.[70]

It is Jesus' obedience to the will of his Father that is the ground of our salvation. It was a full and complete obedience, tested in every way that obedience can be tested. It was to be obedient that Christ became man. Paul indicated this when he summed up Jesus' ministry by saying that he humbled himself, becoming obedient even unto death, yes, the death of the cross.[71] Paul went on immediately to say that because of this obedience Christ has been glorified. His obedience was the victory which has been rewarded with glory and with that name which is above every name, that at the name of Jesus every knee should bow and every tongue confess that Jesus Christ is Lord to the glory of God the Father.[72]

The Epistle to the Hebrews states that it was to be obedient to the will of God that Christ became incarnate and that through the doing of this will he has brought salvation to his people. "'Behold, I have come to do thy will'... By

68 Matt 3:17
69 Col 2:15
70 Heb 2:5-15
71 Phil 2:8
72 Phil 2:8-11

this will we have been sanctified through the offering of the body of Jesus Christ once for all".[73] Christ's obedience to God is the ground of our salvation and its result is the defeat and binding of Satan, and the release of those held captive by him. Forgiveness is the ground of their release. Sin, Satan and the law have no more claim on them.

The New Testament has more than one way of referring to Christ's obedience. One example is the cross of Christ, where the place of his obedience stands for that obedience. Similarly, the death of Christ refers to the manner of his obedience. The blood of Christ is a phrase drawn from Old Testament sacrificial terminology, as is also the description of his death as a sacrifice. Both are metaphors drawn from the worship of the Old Testament to describe what Jesus did on the cross, which is called in Hebrews 13 our altar.[74] In Leviticus 17:11, the blood poured out at the altar covered sin. All sacrifices atoned for sin. Christ is our sacrifice, the cross is our altar, his blood metaphorically poured out in God's presence covers our sins. All these phrases are metaphorical ways of saying that Christ's perfect obedience to the will of God, tested to the full on the cross, makes atonement for sin in his bearing our penalty, fulfilling our obligations and defeating our enemy.

Man's fundamental sin in the Garden of Eden was disobedience and it remains disobedience today. Christ reversed that disobedience, being the first man ever perfectly to obey the will of our heavenly Father and to obey it in every conceivable manner of testing, even that of having our

73 Heb 10:9-10
74 Heb 13:10

sins laid upon him, of being made sin and bearing the curse of separation from God—all of which he bore with perfect obedience and with perfect love towards God, receiving it as the cup which his Father had given him. The contrast between Adam's disobedience and Christ's obedience is very clear in Romans 5, where Paul stated that it is Christ's obedience which is the ground of our justification. "For as through the one man's disobedience the many were made sinners, even so through the *obedience* of the one the many will be made righteous."[75]

All men everywhere should obey God in the daily circumstances of life. None of us is exempt from this ongoing obligation and duty, a pleasurable duty for those who know God as their Father, a duty nevertheless for all those who have been created by God and given life through his goodness. Jesus fulfilled this obedience in his daily living, as we also should. In this sense, he is the exact pattern for us to follow.[76] His obedience and ours are of the same character. Nevertheless, as we have already seen, his obedience went further than we will ever be called upon to obey. The Father asked the Son to obey in bearing the sins of his people. This was the cup which the Father gave him. The content of his obedience was unique, and our Lord accepted it in complete filial obedience, in love and faith. It was a unique obedience—the character the same as our obligation, the content unique. It is the content of his obedience which saves.

It is important to recognize and maintain the distinction between formal obedience to God—a duty which we

75 Rom 5:19
76 1 Pet 2:21-23, 4:1-2

share equally with Christ—and the material obedience of Christ, which was unique to him. A failure to observe this distinction misled the Lambeth Conference Committee into enunciating a doctrine of the Lord's Supper in which the Christian's willing obedience in daily life is the same as the obedience of Christ on the cross which the Lord's Supper commemorates.[77] This confusion leads to an erroneous doctrine of the Lord's Supper, where the supper is thought of as an extension of our Lord's sacrifice instead of a remembrance of it.

Our suffering as Christians may be described as a partaking of the sufferings of Christ.[78] Formally, they are identical, but the content of the suffering is different. Christ suffered by bearing the consequences of justice which a righteous judge awards sinners; we suffer (as Christ also did) by bearing the consequences of injustices which sinners inflict on the righteous. But both are suffering in the cause of righteousness and both, by bearing the suffering in the right way, defeat Satan and roll back his kingdom. In this way we fill up what was lacking in the sufferings of Christ.[79]

The Saviour

Our Lord's obedience was unique and its effect was coextensive with humanity. There is no limitation in the work of our Lord on the cross. What he fulfilled at Calvary he fulfilled for every man. Thus he fulfilled every man's

77 *The Lambeth Conference 1958: The Encyclical Letter from the Bishops together with the Resolutions and Reports*, SPCK, London, 1958, 2.84. For further discussion of this, see DB Knox, 'Some aspects of the atonement', in Tony Payne (ed.), *D. Broughton Knox Selected Works*, vol. 1, *The Doctrine of God*, Matthias Media, Sydney, 2000, pp. 253-266.
78 1 Pet 4:13
79 Col 1:24

obligation to be completely obedient to the will of God. Whatever God wills for us, that is what we must obey. Our Lord obeyed in everything that the Father willed that he should do. Every man is obligated to obey the will of God. Jesus obeyed in everything; his obedience was complete. He could not have obeyed more completely, more perfectly, whether he was bearing the sin of one man only or of an immense multitude. Thus Christ fulfilled every man's obligation to walk in all the things written in the book of the law to do them.[80]

Secondly, Jesus bore every man's penalty. Every man deserves, and all outside of Christ will receive, the penalty of separation from God, of being cast out into outer darkness, of partaking of the everlasting punishment prepared for the devil and his angels.[81] That is what each one of us in ourselves deserves, and that is what our Lord endured. God laid on him the sin of us all. There are no depths of penalty that could be added to what our Lord underwent. His obedience was tested to the full; his sinbearing was complete. He drank the cup of God's wrath against sin to the dregs,[82] and he drank it without any breach of faith or trust or love in the God who was giving it to him to drink, who was laying on him the iniquity of us all. Thus our Lord bore every man's penalty, the punishment that every man deserves. It is impossible to conceive of the limitation of our Lord's work on the cross, as though he would have borne more suffering, more punishment had his merits been applied in the mind

80 Gal 3:10
81 2 Thess 1:9; Matt 25:41
82 Ps 75:8

and purpose of God to more sinners. The atonement is not quantitative, as though God added up the sins of the elect and placed the penalty for these and these only on Jesus; but the atonement is qualitative. Our Lord experienced fully the penalty for sin.

Thirdly, on the cross our Lord overcame every man's enemy. He brought to nought the devil who keeps every man in subjection through fear of death.[83] Viewed from this angle, once again it is seen that our Lord's death on Calvary and what he accomplished there are coextensive with humanity. All are enslaved to Satan, who is the strong man who through the fear of death keeps us all in bondage. He is the strong man whom Jesus, the stronger, has bound and whose goods he is now spoiling at his own discretion.[84]

Thus Jesus discharged every man's obligation to keep the law. He bore every man's penalty of separation from God. He overcame and bound every man's enemy, the devil. The redemption our Lord achieved on Calvary was unlimited with regard to humanity—he took every man's nature; he underwent every man's curse; he fulfilled every man's obligation; he overcame every man's enemy. There is no limit in the provision of forgiveness which Jesus achieved at Calvary. All the children of Adam may share it if they call upon the name of the Lord.

Christ commanded his disciples to proclaim forgiveness of sins in his name throughout the world.[85] There is provision of salvation for every hearer of the gospel. For if

83 Heb 2:14
84 Mark 3:27
85 Luke 24:47

there were no provision for some, there could be no offer of salvation to these; and if there is no genuine offer, there is no responsibility or blame in rejecting the offer, indeed, only commendation for not being taken in by a spurious invitation to come to Christ for salvation, which in fact is not available. But there is provision of salvation for everyone who hears the gospel. It was made by Christ on Calvary, when he gave his flesh for the life of the world,[86] and so became the Saviour of the world.[87]

Jesus' faithfulness is our salvation

We have seen that the New Testament ascribes our Lord's achievement of our salvation to his obedience: "Through the obedience of the one shall the many be made righteous".[88] Now obedience is the overt expression of faith. Faith and obedience are closely linked. They are in fact one concept. Faithfulness to God is only another way of saying obedience to God. To put faith in God is expressed outwardly by obeying God, that is why James said in his letter, "I will show you my faith by my works".[89] A person who says that he believes, yet does not obey, is deceiving himself. We may therefore put the matter of our salvation in more than one way. We may say that we are saved by our Lord's death, as is so frequently said in the New Testament, or that we are saved by our Lord's obedience, as in Romans 5, Philippians 2 and Hebrews 10. Or again we may say that we are saved by our Lord's faith expressed in faithfulness to God.

86 John 6:51
87 1 John 4:14
88 Rom 5:19
89 Jas 2:18

Now Jesus' faith is frequently mentioned in the New Testament as the ground of our salvation, but this has not been noticed in the English translations. The phrase "the faith of our Lord Jesus Christ" is normally interpreted in the English versions of the Bible as our faith *in* Jesus Christ. The Greek can mean this. But the contexts show that it ought to be understood and translated in a more straightforward way as the *faith* or the *faithfulness* of Jesus Christ, that is to say, the obedience of Jesus Christ. An example is Galatians 3:22. This reads in the Revised Version, "that the promise by faith in Jesus Christ might be given to them that believe". It makes better sense and removes the double reference to believing if the Greek is translated more exactly: "That the promise based on the faithfulness of Jesus Christ might be given to them that believe". In Philippians 3:9, there is again a double reference to faith which is tautological in the normal English translations but which becomes full of significance when we realize that the first reference to faith is to the faith or faithfulness of Jesus, while the second reference is to our faith in him. Thus it should be translated: "The righteousness which is through the faithfulness of Christ, that is, the righteousness which comes from God upon our faith".

Similarly in Romans 3:22, the text in the Revised Version reads, "the righteousness of God through faith in Jesus Christ unto all them that believe". Once again, it makes better sense of the Greek, as well as theologically, if it is translated, "the righteousness of God through the faithfulness of Jesus Christ unto all them that believe". The phrase "the righteousness of God" expresses the truth that God gives believers in Jesus the status of being righteous, and this gift of God is based on the faithfulness, that is, the obedience of Jesus Christ in life and death, and it is given to all who believe in Jesus as Lord. That is the meaning of the sentence, and is in conformity with the rest of the teaching of the New Testament. However, this meaning is lost when it is translated in the customary way.

A similar consideration applies to the translation of that famous verse Romans 1:17, where Paul sums up the gospel. It is normally translated, "The righteousness of God from faith to faith", a phrase to which it is difficult to give any real sense—a fact witnessed by the various paraphrastic translations attempted in the modern English versions. However, the meaning becomes crystal clear when it is seen that the first reference to faith is to Jesus' faith and the second reference is to the faith which we in response exercise towards him. In this sentence the apostle states that the gospel is the news of a righteousness which comes from God by way of gift, based on the faithfulness of Jesus, and is given to those who have faith in Jesus as Lord. Interpreted thus, the verse makes very good sense both grammatically and theologically.

It may be that the reason why what is plain in the Greek has never been expressed in the translations is that a very long tradition in theology has upheld that it is impossible for the incarnate Son of God to exercise faith because, being God, he is omniscient. But, as we have already seen, the Scripture makes clear that Jesus did not share the omniscience of God in his human life, but that his knowledge was based on his relationship to the Father and on the Father's will. Therefore there was room for faith. Indeed, Scripture reveals that Jesus lived the life of faith and describes him as "the prince and perfecter of faith".[90] It also makes clear that it is our Lord's faith which is the ground of our salvation. God's gift of righteousness, without which we cannot stand in his presence, is based on Christ's work which may be summed up either as his obedience or as his faithfulness. The words 'faith' and 'faithfulness' are, of course, the same word in the Greek because the concepts are identical.

Our faith in Jesus, by which we are saved, is closely linked to his faith in God, which is the ground of our salvation. It is wonderful to think that by exercising faith in Christ we are walking in the footsteps of our Saviour, working the same work of God, which won from his Father the encomium: "In you I am well pleased".[91] We fill up, as it were, in our own body that which is lacking in the sufferings of Christ, as we live our daily life in faith in the same way as the Saviour walked the path of faith before us. He is our example of faith, as Hebrews 12:2 puts it.

Coming on the clouds to the throne[92]

On account of his victory on the cross, Jesus is exalted to God's right hand, which is the symbol of rule and government. He has received the kingdom which Daniel 7 foretold was to be given to the Son of Man who, coming in the clouds of heaven to the Ancient of Days, would receive the kingdom on behalf of the people of God, a kingdom which would be without end. The passage in Daniel reads,

90 Heb 12:2
91 Matt 3:17, 12:18, 17:5
92 For an exposition of the different 'comings' of Jesus and their meaning, see DB Knox, 'The five comings of Jesus (Matthew 24 and 25)', in Tony Payne (ed.), *D Broughton Knox Selected Works*, vol. 1, *The Doctrine of God*, Matthias Media, Sydney, 2000, pp. 213-227.

I kept looking in the night visions,
And behold, with the clouds of heaven
One like a Son of Man was coming
And he came up to the Ancient of Days
and was presented before him.
And to him was given dominion,
Glory and a kingdom,
that all the peoples, nations and men of every language
Might serve him.
His dominion is an everlasting dominion
Which will not pass away;
And his kingdom is one
Which will not be destroyed.[93]

The vision is interpreted at the end of the chapter thus: "The kingdom, the dominion, and the greatness of all the kingdoms under the whole heaven will be given to the people of the saints of the Highest One; his kingdom will be an everlasting kingdom, and all dominions will serve and obey him".[94] This prophecy was repeated at the annunciation[95] and was fulfilled at the ascension.[96] Jesus had referred to its fulfilment several times during his ministry. In his Olivet discourse, he predicted (with great emphasis on the reliability of his prediction) that the generation who heard him would not pass away until they had seen the Son of Man coming in the clouds with great power and glory.[97] To the Sanhedrin, a day or so later, he predicted that from that

93 Dan 7:13-14
94 Dan 7:27
95 Luke 1:32-33
96 Matt 28:16-20
97 Mark 13:26, 30

time onwards they would see the Son of Man seated at the right hand of God and coming with the clouds.[98] "To come with the clouds" is a reference to the prophecy of Daniel, that the Son of Man would come with the clouds to the throne of God and receive the kingdom, a prophecy fulfilled through the cross and symbolized in its fulfilment by the ascension, when our Lord ascended in the clouds to heaven and to his throne.

This "coming with the clouds" to the Father's right hand to receive the kingdom at the ascension is to be distinguished from the coming of the Son of Man at the end of the world when he will come in the glory of his Father with the holy angels to sit on his throne of judgement.[99] The coming in the clouds was fulfilled, as Jesus predicted, within that generation. But the time of the coming of the Son of Man in judgement at the end of the world, on 'that day' as the New Testament phrase has it, has not been made known. The Father has kept that time within his own power,[100] so naturally our Lord made no prediction as to when it would be. The confusion between the coming with the clouds to the Father's throne, predicted in Daniel and fulfilled at the ascension, and the coming to his judgement throne in flaming fire at the end of the world, has led to a great deal of misunderstanding of what is otherwise the plain text of Scripture. Both comings are foretold in Daniel 7, for Jesus is the Son of Man, coming in the clouds to the throne, and he is also the Ancient of Days, coming in fire with his holy angels for judgement.[101]

98 Mark 14:62
99 Mark 8:38; cf. Matt 25:31
100 Acts 1:7
101 Dan 7:9-10, 21-22

Coming in judgement

The judgement on the final day will be judgement by the Son of Man. Jesus described how, in that day, the Son of Man will come in his glory and all the angels with him, and he will sit on the throne of his glory with the nations gathered before him for judgement.[102] Judgement is from eternity associated with the Son. Jesus told the Jews, "For not even the Father judges anyone, but he has given all judgement to the Son",[103] and again, "he gave him authority to execute judgement, because he is the Son of Man".[104]

The judgements of God are not restricted to the last day but have been experienced throughout history. Just as the final judgement will be that of the Son of Man in his day, so these earlier judgements which humanity has experienced are "days of the Son of Man".[105] Judgement means the vindication of the right, and the righteous rejoice when they see the judgement of God. As Psalm 98 puts it, "Sing joyfully to Yahweh, all the earth... let the mountains sing together for joy before Yahweh, for he is coming to judge the earth; he will judge the world with righteousness and the peoples with equity".[106]

Jesus foretold that the days would come when the disciples would long for vindication of righteousness through judgement, but they would not experience it, for it was not then God's time. He said, "The days shall come when you will long to see one of the days of the Son of Man,

102 Matt 25:31
103 John 5:22
104 John 5:27
105 Luke 17:22
106 Ps 98:4, 8-9

and you will not see it".[107] 'Day' is a New Testament term for judgement, as the Greek of 1 Corinthians 4:3 makes clear.[108] Abraham had seen one of those days of the Son of Man when, rising early in the morning and standing on the place where he had met the Lord the day before, "he looked down toward Sodom and Gomorrah, and toward all the land of the valley, and he saw, and behold, the smoke of the land ascended like the smoke of a furnace".[109] God's judgement on Sodom was the coming, the *parousia*, the regal presence of the Son of Man.[110] It was "one of the days of the Son of Man" for the Father has given all judgement to the Son.

The destruction of Jerusalem was an even more signal day of the Son of Man, when the blood of the innocent, from the blood of righteous Abel to that of righteous Zechariah, was required by God at the hands of the inhabitants of Jerusalem in a tribulation which has never been exceeded.[111] It was a day when God was present in judgement, a day of the *parousia* of the Son of Man. Like all the comings of the Son of Man, it was as sudden and as clear as a lightning flash,[112] or as when eagles swoop upon a carcass.[113]

The judgements of the Son of Man are never expected by the recipients. People go on their way eating and drinking, marrying and giving in marriage until the flood of

107 Luke 17:22
108 1 Corinthans 4:3 reads, literally: "But with me it is a very small thing that I should be judged by you, or by any human *day*".
109 Gen 19:27-28
110 cf. John 8:56—"Your father Abraham rejoiced to see my day; and he saw it, and was glad."
111 Matt 23:35
112 Luke 17:24
113 Luke 17:37

judgement comes and destroys them all.[114] So, too, the final denouement in the day when the Son of Man is revealed will be unexpected by all except those who are waiting for it.

Kingdom and dominion

At the creation, God purposed that the dominion should be given to mankind. The New Testament sees this purpose of God as fulfilled in Jesus, in the dominion that he received through the cross at his ascension. 1 Corinthians 15, Ephesians 1 and Hebrews 2 make it clear that the Genesis narrative, taken up in Psalm 8, is fulfilled in Jesus of Nazareth. He is the One to whom all things have been subjected. God's purposes for mankind have been fulfilled in him and in those who are in him. He is not only the image of God, as we have already seen, but he is the One to whom dominion has been given and so the words of Genesis are fulfilled: "Let us make man in our image after our likeness and let them have dominion".[115] On two occasions Jesus taught his disciples that the dominion had been given to him. He began his prayer on the eve of his crucifixion with the words: "Father… [you] gave [the Son] *authority over all mankind*, that to all whom you have given him, he may give eternal life".[116] And on the eve of his ascension he assured his disciples, "*All authority has been given to me in heaven and earth*. Go therefore and make disciples of all the nations."[117]

Salvation comes to sinners by their acknowledgement of this dominion of Jesus. To acknowledge Jesus as Lord is

114 Matt 24:38
115 Gen 1:26
116 John 17:2
117 Matt 28:18-19

the touchstone of being a Christian.[118] When in the New Testament it is said that salvation comes through faith in Jesus, it means faith in Jesus as Lord. That lordship was accomplished on the cross so that his Lordship and his saviourhood are identical concepts. He saves by victory over sin through bearing sin perfectly, and all sinners who call upon him as the victorious Lord will be saved. Our acknowledgement of the dominion of Christ does not only look back to Calvary, though that is its basis, but it takes in its scope the present and the future also. His dominion is exercised at the present moment. He is reigning and must reign, says Paul, until every enemy is put under his feet.[119]

The dominion of God is a very different sort of dominion from what we understand by the word in ordinary human relationships. As Jesus pointed out, the nations of the world exercise dominion over one another by force.[120] Had Jesus' dominion been of that sort, were his kingdom of this world, his disciples would doubtless have used force to protect and extend his kingdom or rule. But the dominion of God is a dominion which flows from righteousness and love. This is how God exercises his dominion in heaven and therefore also on earth. In heaven, the will of God is done because those who are there love God and love the rightness of God's will. God exercises his dominion through the glad obedience of perfect hearts. Christ in his earthly life followed and expressed this kingdom or dominion of God. In heaven, it is unalloyed joy to express the kingdom of God. In this sinful

118 Rom 10:9; cf. 1 Cor 12:3
119 1 Cor 15:25
120 Matt 20:25

world, the joy is mingled with suffering—suffering at the hands of sinners—but it is also the occasion for victory over sin, and so the extension of the dominion or kingdom of God. Christians share the dominion of Christ. "They reign upon the earth" as the best manuscript of the book of the Revelation puts it.[121] The Christian's reign upon the earth is a present reality. And like their master, their exercise of the dominion of God, their expression of God's kingdom will involve them in victory. Satan the prince of this world will be repulsed, and the kingdom or dominion of God, God's rule, will be extended. Their faith (which is expressed in their obedience) is the victory which overcomes the world.[122]

The lordship of Christ is manifested not only in the past at Calvary, and in the present through the victory that his servants win by suffering righteously in this world of sin, but it will also be manifested at the Last Day. Consequently the acknowledgement of Jesus as Lord comprises not only the past and present, but also looks forward to the future. That future look was very characteristic of Christians of the New Testament. They were awaiting their Lord from heaven.[123] They lived by hope, as we should, too. Their expectation was put very vividly by Paul in his second letter to the Thessalonians when he spoke of

> your perseverance and faith in the midst of all your persecutions and afflictions which you endure. This is a plain indication of God's righteous judgement so that you may be considered worthy of the kingdom of God,

121 Rev 5:10
122 1 John 5:4
123 1 Thess 1:10

> for which indeed you are suffering. For after all it is only just for God to repay with affliction those who afflict you, and to give relief to you who are afflicted and to us as well when the Lord Jesus shall be revealed from heaven with his mighty angels in flaming fire, dealing out retribution to those who do not know God and to those who do not obey the gospel of our Lord Jesus. And these will pay the penalty of eternal destruction, away from the presence of the Lord and from the glory of his power, when he comes to be glorified in his saints on that day, and to be marvelled at among all who have believed.[124]

All this is included in the belief that saves. For Jesus is Lord, Lord of the future, as well as Lord of the present and the past. The apostles told the Philippian gaoler, "Believe in the *Lord*, Jesus, and you shall be saved, you and your household".[125]

124 2 Thess 1:4-10
125 Acts 16:31

chapter 5

God who is rich in mercy

'The everlasting purpose of God to deliver those whom he has chosen in Christ'[1]

The subject of predestination is one that often puzzles Christians. The question of how to think about predestination is an important one; it affects our whole attitude to life and salvation and to our trust and joy in God. The doctrine of predestination is simple to state. It is that from eternity God has chosen some for salvation in Christ, but has left others to their own choice of rebellion against him. On some he has mercy, drawing them to Christ; others he has hardened by allowing them to harden themselves, or rather to be hardened and blinded by Satan, whose slaves they have willingly become.

We do not by nature like the doctrine of predestination, for it appears to make us puppets on the one hand, and it appears unfair on the other. Yet it is a doctrine that is amply taught in Holy Scripture. It is based on the nature of God, who is sovereign and merciful; it is based on the nature of men, rebellious and dead in sin; and it is based on the character of salvation, which is a free gift.

The basic concept of the Christian faith is that God is gracious. This is clearly revealed in the Old Testament when

1 This opening quotation is from the Anglican Thirty-nine Articles, article 17, 'Of Predestination and Election'.

God declared his character to the children of Israel in the early days of the desert wanderings: "Yahweh, the God Yahweh, compassionate and gracious, slow to anger, and abounding in lovingkindness and truth; who keeps lovingkindness for thousands, who forgives iniquity, transgression and sin".[2] God's tender mercies are over all his works.[3] The love of God is the motive for salvation: "God so loved the world, that he gave his only begotten Son".[4]

But an equally important truth to remember (and one that we are much more ready to forget) is that God is Creator of everything, and sovereign Lord over all that he has created. His sovereign lordship is not only over the impersonal happenings of nature but also over the lives of men and women, who are a part of his creation. His sovereignty in our lives is not exercised in an impersonal way, but through our natures that he himself has made. To think that God has withdrawn from any area and given over his sovereignty would be an unbearable thought. To think that God is unable to remain sovereign, having created men and women with true human natures and human wills, is, of course, absurd. The Bible teaches clearly, and common sense confirms, that God is sovereign over every aspect of his creation, over the great and over the minute, over men and women, their actions, thoughts and wills, and even over evil men and their wills.[5] He is sovereign over death—he can bring the dead to life by his word as easily as he brought creation into existence out of nothingness in the first

2 Exod 34:6-7
3 Ps 145:9
4 John 3:16
5 See chapter 2.

place. His sovereignty is not diminished because of man's rebellion against him.

Alongside the goodness of God and the lordship of God, the Bible places the rectitude of God. He is upright in his thoughts and actions and he has implanted the same sense of rectitude in our minds and consciences. We approve righteousness and justice, and the Bible is very clear that God approves righteousness and justice. He is the vindicator of the right, and the awarder of rewards and punishments in accordance with desert. How frequently we read in the Bible that God will judge every man according to his works![6]

It is here that the human problem becomes acute. Our own sense of rectitude and our own conscience tell us that we do things which deserve not reward but punishment. Our future is a fearful expectation of judgement whenever we remember that God is righteous and sovereign, and that he will judge the whole creation in righteousness and truth. God's rectitude will ensure that justice and right are vindicated. Our problem is that in a world where justice will be vindicated we are unjust. The Bible is clear that there is none of us righteous, no not one; we have all turned aside,[7] we are all under God's condemnation and without power of self recovery. None of us can be saved unless God saves us. As Jesus said, "No man can come to me, unless the Father who sent me draws him".[8] As Jeremiah put it, "Can the Ethiopian change his skin, or the leopard his spots? Then you also can do good who are accustomed to do evil".[9] Or, in Paul's words,

6 For example, Romans 2:6; 2 Timothy 4:14.
7 Rom 3:10-12
8 John 6:44
9 Jer 13:23

"The mind of the flesh is hostile towards God; for it does not subject itself to the law of God, for it is not even able to do so; and those who are in the flesh cannot please God".[10] Because we choose to do what we know to be wrong, God gives us up to our choice. That is fair, but it means hell for all of us; it means eternal separation from God; it means the outer darkness where there is weeping and gnashing of teeth. There is no difference; all have sinned.[11] By disobedience, we all cut ourselves off from God, the source of life. We have involved ourselves in death—in physical death—but more importantly in spiritual and eternal death. We are dead, says Paul, in our trespasses and sins.[12] We are by nature children of wrath, under God's eternal condemnation of death. Dead people cannot save themselves. We need new life, a completely new start, a new creation, as it were, a spiritual resurrection, a new birth, as Jesus told Nicodemus.[13] And it is God, the Creator, the sovereign Lord, who alone can bring about this radical change and this new start, this new creation, this spiritual resurrection. We must be born by the power of God's Spirit.[14] The doctrine of predestination is simply the consequence of man's nature (dead in trespasses and sins), and of God's nature (goodness and mercy), and of his sovereignty and power, through which he recreates those who are dead in their sins, to be his sons and daughters, choosing according to his own wise and loving and righteous will.

10 Rom 8:7-8
11 Rom 3:22-23
12 Eph 2:1-3
13 John 3:3
14 John 3:5-8

The biblical foundation

Passages of Scripture which teach the doctrine of election and predestination are many. One or two illustrations will suffice. Paul wrote,

> He [God] chose us in him [Christ] before the foundation of the world, that we should be holy and blameless before him. In love he predestined us to adoption as sons through Jesus Christ to himself, according to the kind intention of his will, to the praise of his grace, which he freely bestowed on us in the beloved… In him also we have obtained an inheritance, having been predestined according to his purpose who works all things after the counsel of his will, to the end that we who were the first to hope in Christ should be to the praise of his glory.[15]

In 2 Thessalonians 2:13-14 the apostle wrote, "God has chosen you from the beginning for salvation through sanctification by the Spirit and faith in the truth. And it was for this he called you through our gospel, that you may gain the glory of our Lord Jesus Christ." Peter wrote his letter to those whom he described as having been "chosen according to the foreknowledge of God the Father".[16] Luke described the result of the preaching of Paul and Barnabas with the words: "As many as had been appointed to eternal life believed".[17] Likewise Paul wrote, "God causes all things to work together for good to those who love God, to those who are called according to his purpose. For whom he foreknew,

15 Eph 1:4-12
16 1 Pet 1:1-2
17 Acts 13:48

he also predestined to become conformed to the image of his son."[18] But it is in the next chapter, Romans 9, that Paul wrote most fully on the doctrine of predestination. First, he stated that God chose Jacob rather than Esau simply because of God's own decision. There was nothing in the children which evoked that choice. The apostle concluded, "He has mercy on whom he desires, and he hardens whom he desires".[19] Then in the rest of the chapter the apostle made clear by the way he answered objections that God's choice is not conditioned by anything in those who are predestined.

The intellectual problem

The doctrine of predestination provides an intellectual as well as an ethical problem. The intellectual problem is that of the relationship of our wills, which we know to be real wills, with the sovereign will of God who chooses for salvation. The ethical problem is the question of the fairness of God's choice: why one and not the other?

First let us look at the problem of the intellect—the relationship of the will of God and our wills. This problem of the relationship of the supreme will of Almighty God and the subordinate but real wills of men and women is a difficult one, because there is no parallel in our experience to help us understand it. Our imagination finds difficulty in comprehending how our wills, which we know to be real, can remain true wills within the sovereign will of our Creator, in whom we live and move and have our being[20]

18 Rom 8:28-29
19 Rom 9:18
20 Acts 17:28

and who, so we are clearly taught by revelation, works all things after the counsel of his will.[21] Philosophical theology stumbles over the problem, but there is no problem within the experience of the converted, regenerate Christian. For example, the Christian who is in personal fellowship with his heavenly Father prays with complete confidence to God for guidance through the intricacies of life. In this, he is following numerous spiritual injunctions to commit his way to the Lord who will direct his paths. As the Christian looks back over life, he can see clearly that God has fulfilled and is fulfilling his promise to answer this prayer for guidance, yet the guidance experienced comes through entirely natural means. At no point is the Christian conscious that his own natural God-given faculties are suspended in order that the guidance might be piped to him, as it were. Every step of the road is his step, every decision is his, made, if he has these particular gifts, by intellectual reflection and decision, otherwise perhaps through the influence of friends and their intellectual wisdom. Thus the Christian is conscious both of the over-ruling guidance of God and of the true and full working of his own nature and of circumstance in the receiving of this guidance. Reason may find difficulty in reconciling these two but experience finds none.

Or take another illustration from the field of human relations. The Christian does not hesitate to pray for divine protection from external dangers, whether through natural forces or from malevolent people. He is conscious that God is able to restrain human wrath; indeed if God did not do this, who would survive? Thus the Christian prays with

21 Eph 1:11

confidence that God will protect him, for it never enters his mind to think that the answer to his prayer might be that God has limited his authority because he has given humanity free will, and that therefore the supplication should be directed to the malevolent person rather than to Almighty God.

In these two areas of Christian experience we have examples of the relationship between the free will of man and the sovereign will of God. God is sovereign, yet the reality of our nature and our free will is not infringed. The Scripture abounds with examples. Thus Joseph answered his brothers, "It is not you who sent me here, but God";[22] and "You meant evil against me, but God meant it for good".[23] Every action which led to Joseph's position in Egypt was God's action. God sent him to Egypt, yet at the same time it remained truly human action, freely decided on, so that those who perpetrated the wrong remained responsible.

Job's reply to his misfortunes has always been recognized not only as very pious, but also as very true: "Yahweh gave, and Yahweh has taken away".[24] The ultimate truth was that the Lord Yahweh took away Job's possessions, for the Lord was in complete control of the Chaldeans and the other brigands who, inflamed by greed and lust for loot, destroyed Job's servants and drove off his livestock.[25] The Lord was not only in complete control of the brigands and all their actions, which they freely undertook and which sprang from their evil natures, but he also controlled the maliciousness

22 Gen 45:8
23 Gen 50:20
24 Job 1:21
25 Job 1:13-17

of their demonic master, setting strict limits to his actions,[26] which his wicked nature originated.

On the day of Pentecost Peter told the Jerusalem crowd, "you nailed [him] to a cross by the hands of godless men and put him to death".[27] These men acted freely according to their own lawless natures. But everything that happened was, as Peter put it, according to the "predetermined plan and foreknowledge of God".[28] Similarly, the first Christians acknowledged in their prayer that Herod and Pontius Pilate with the Gentiles and the people of Israel were gathered together to do "whatever your hand and your purpose predestined to occur".[29] From the point of view of history, the crucifixion was just an ordinary event indistinguishable from any other. It was the result of the ordinary interaction of men and women. But the Bible sees every detail as pre-ordained by God's predetermined plan. What is true of Calvary is true of every event everywhere throughout human history.

Free will

The problem of the relationship of God's will to the created will is not to be solved by denying God's sovereignty, as though through the creation of human wills and demonic wills he had delimited an area within his creation over which he had given up control. Not only is this contrary to the whole of revelation, but it would be unbearable and terrifying were it true, and prayer and trust would become impossible. God has not limited himself in any way at all.

26 Job 1:12
27 Acts 2:23
28 Acts 2:23
29 Acts 4:27-28

The Bible knows nothing of such an idea.

Nor is the problem of the relationship of God's will and ours to be solved by denying the reality of the human will, as though it were not what we experience it to be, namely a true will. The word 'free' adds nothing to the meaning of the word 'will', and the denial of the word 'free' is meaningless, so long as we are talking about what we experience as will, which is the only will of which we have direct knowledge. Although our wills are free wills, it is incorrect to say that they are independent wills over against God's will. The possibility of this concept was the false suggestion of the devil to Adam, grasped at by man but certainly not achieved by him, though man thinks he has attained to it and that he is in fact free from God's sovereignty. Adam's mistake was that of thinking that by rebelling against God he would become sovereign. But no creature can ever become sovereign over against its almighty Creator, and no will can be free if by this is meant independent of its Creator.

The regenerate man does not wish to have a will operative outside the sphere of God's sovereignty. The concept is repulsive. The unregenerate man may desire this, but he certainly does not possess it. The poet may inveigh,

> It matters not how strait the gate,
> How charged with punishments the scroll,
> I am the master of my fate,
> I am the captain of my soul.[30]

But his sentiments are baseless. This attitude of independence of man over against God is what the natural man

30 William Ernest Henley, *Invictus*, 1875.

would like. It is what Adam grasped at, but it is a chimera. Sin does not remove us from God's sovereignty, otherwise sin would be a tremendous success. God remains sovereign; we remain true men and women, enslaved now to the devil against our nature, instead of to our true Master, but nevertheless still within the sovereignty of God who is Lord over heaven and hell. It sounds good to boast against heaven, "I am the master of my fate, I am the captain of my soul", but it is false. God controls his creation; he does not originate moral evil or sin, for this originates from the created will (or rather, person), yet he remains in control of its effects. He is also able to re-create the will and free it from sin, in accordance with his own decision and choice.

The freedom, that is to say, the reality of our will, is not infringed by God's sovereignty, because he exercises his sovereignty only in accordance with the natures of his creation. Thus in working in us he works through our natures, which he has created, and which he foresaw in determining his plan, indeed which he created for the purpose of fulfilling his decrees. Thus God's working out his sovereign will appears to us entirely natural, that is to say, in accordance with the nature of things, as in the case of God's guidance and protection. The problem of reconciling God's sovereignty and the reality of our will remains with the intellect, but it is not a problem of experience or of revelation, which is clear and unwavering on the subject.

Perseverance

Although converted Christians do not differ among themselves on the reality of God's guidance and protection, there has been strong controversy about the sovereignty of God in the transformation of the rebellious sinner into a son of God, into a new creation in Christ, and his perseverance to the end. Yet it must be said that there does not seem to be any real room for denying that the testimony of Scripture is overwhelmingly in support of the sovereignty of God in all aspects of salvation as in every other sphere of human affairs.

It is sometimes argued that the exhortations and especially the admonitions and warnings of Scripture are a proof that there is a real possibility that God's elect will fall away and fail to persevere to the end. This is to misunderstand the purpose of these exhortations and warnings. God works through our natures so that in bringing his children to glory he will work with them through their response to his Word. Their regenerate wills will gladly follow his exhortations and take heed to the warnings. It always remains true that if a person continues in sin he will not inherit the kingdom of God. Paul reiterated warnings that fornicators and drunkards and idolators and moneymakers will not inherit the kingdom of God.[31] This remains true. All of us know that we can at any time choose to give ourselves to these things and so fall away and be lost eternally. Indeed, left to ourselves, it is certain that we will fall into one or the other of these sinful ways of life. Nevertheless, by the grace of God we do not, for the warnings are the means by which God saves us from these fatal falls, just as the warning erected in front of a precipice is effective to prevent anybody falling over. The warning notice does not mean that someone must have fallen down the precipice before it was erected, or that

31 1 Cor 6:9; Gal 5:21

someone will fall over in the future, but it simply indicates that if you ignore the warning you will be killed; however, no-one need ignore it. Indeed, no-one will who reads it. So too in Holy Scripture the warnings are to ensure our perseverance and they achieve this.

Salvation is through faith, which is expressed in obedience. Now faith and obedience are the work of our own personality, but are also the work of God in the heart of the believer. God works through our natures, and in his working he does not destroy or suspend these natures, nor do the natures get in the way of his working. It must always be remembered that God works out his purposes through the nature of his creatures. He does not find the nature which he has created an obstruction to his will. Thus he has created men and women with responsible natures and true wills. In calling his elect and bringing them to glory God does not need to suspend our nature or overrule our will, but he accomplishes his purposes, determined on before the creation of the world, through our free will.

So faith and obedience are both the work of God and at the same time our own work. Since faith is the work of man we must preach the gospel and exhort people to believe, and must ourselves believe and persevere in our obedience; yet since it is a work of God we must look to God, trust him that he will give faith according to his will, and give him thanks when we see evidence of that creative will; for ourselves, we must rely on his faithfulness to keep us to the end, according to his promises. In the case of the unregenerate hearer of the gospel the warnings and promises are not indications of an ability to respond, for they are disbelieved and ignored through sin. Yet they remain indications of reality. The warning is true and the promise is true. When God creates once again our natures, then we both believe the promises and act on the warnings, and they are the instruments by which God brings his children, whom he has chosen, to his eternal home. Warnings are quite compatible with confident assurance of ultimate salvation. Indeed, these warnings and the careful attention to duty that ensues, are the means of obtaining that salvation.

Take two simple illustrations from current life. The driver of a motor vehicle has confidence that he will attain his destination, but at the same time he remains fully vigilant and he is aware that if, for example, he goes to sleep at the wheel he will be killed. His care and wakefulness in no sense diminish his confidence but are the grounds for it. The warnings alert him so that he avoids the dangers which they indicate. Or, again, in space travel an awareness of the frightful dangers and the inevitable death that would follow even one careless slip does not diminish the confidence of the astronauts in the successful completion of their mission. Vigilance against known dangers, and warnings which make these dangers known, are simply the means of ensuring the successful completion of the mission. They do not reflect any lack of confidence of success, neither is there any need for an accident to take place to make the warnings real and true. So, too, with the warnings of Scripture. There do not need to be any apostates, any of God's true children failing to attain, for the warnings in the Scripture against apostasy to be real and true.

Assurance

The Christian's perseverance rests on the character of God,

and the Christian's assurance of his salvation rests on that character being known to him through God's promises of faithfulness. The Christian is confident that he will not come to grief, and that no-one will pluck him out of his Father's hand.[32] His confidence is well based and will be justified, for God is faithful and almighty.[33] Yet the Christian knows full well that were he to turn away from God, or were he to fail to do what is necessary, for example, in the buffeting of his body, he would be lost.[34] So we can expect to discover in the New Testament the fullest confidence in the sureness of salvation, along with the clearest warnings against the dangers of drifting away. For these warnings are the instrument by which God makes real and actual that sure salvation. The Christian's assurance of perseverance flows from his realization of the faithfulness of God, who will continue the work which he has begun. Yet every Christian at the same time knows that no fornicator or unclean person will inherit the kingdom of God, so he buffets his body lest he become such and so be a castaway. The two concepts of faith in God's faithfulness to keep souls which we have committed to him, and of diligence to make our election sure,[35] fit together like a hand in a glove. They are not in contrast or apparent contradiction, but complement each other, for it is God who works in us as we work.[36]

It is a fatal misunderstanding to think that full assurance of final perseverance is incompatible with warnings

32 John 10:29
33 1 Cor 1:9; 1 Thess 5:23-24
34 1 Cor 9:27
35 2 Pet 1:10
36 Phil 2:12-13

and exhortations against falling away, and to take the occurrence of such warnings and exhortations in Scripture as proof that the writers of Scripture did not believe in predestination and final perseverance, even when they explicitly said that this was their belief. Equally it is a mistake to believe that the will is free against its own Creator. That is the attitude of rebellious man, but it is not true in reality. We cannot be free against our Creator, nor should we wish it. It is sufficient for us if we are free against the influence of all that is not God. As sinners we are very far from free in this respect; we are always slaves to our passions and led captive by the devil. But restored in Christ, we become free in the only way a creature can be free—that is, free to follow its God-given nature; not free against the Giver, but only truly free when it is responding to the overwhelming grace of God, as our natures were created to do.

The ethical problem

The ethical problem in the doctrine of predestination arises from our God-given sense of fairness. Fairness, righteousness and justice are the basis of all our relationships with one another. But we are on dangerous ground if we set up our sense of fairness, that is to say, what we believe to be due to us and to others, as the criterion for judging God's dealings with his rebellious creation. A rebel *deserves* nothing but condemnation and condign punishment. Since salvation, however, is in the realm of mercy, not punishment, it is difficult to see how the concept of fairness plays any part in it. If God is to be fair and just to rebels we all deserve and will receive punishment. But mercy supervenes, and mercy is apart from the realm of justice. In fact, the two concepts are mutually exclusive. That which is deserved is not mercy but reward. Mercy is that which is held out and given to those who have absolutely no claim on it. Consequently the rebellious sinner who is the recipient of God's mercy can hardly discuss and make demands about this mercy on the basis of his sense of fairness.

Mercy is a completely different category from justice. The Lord's parable of the labourers in the vineyard warns us against the fatal error of impugning God's goodness in seeking to judge his acts of mercy and overflowing benevolence by our judgement of what is fair.[37] The Judge of all the earth will do right[38]—of that we may be sure—but he will not be judged by us. It is a very dangerous activity for us to set up as a criterion our sense of what it is fair for him to do to rebels in his distribution of his unmerited mercy, especially when the results of this judgement of ours fly in the face of the overwhelming testimony of revelation.

The Bible constantly testifies that salvation and eternal life are God's gifts.[39] Now a gift is in the complete disposal of the giver; he may give it, or he need not. The same is true of mercy. It is completely at the disposal of the merciful. He may show mercy, or he need not. Salvation is a gift. The Giver may give it, or he need not. If salvation is deserved, it ceases to be a gift. It then becomes reward for merit, wages which have been earned. But salvation is entirely a gift from beginning to end. It therefore means that it must be given according to God's will and choice. The character

37 Matt 20:1-16
38 Gen 18:25
39 For example, John 10:28; Romans 6:23.

of salvation as a gift, the merciful provision of salvation, is bound up with the doctrine of God's complete freedom in election and predestination.

In Christ

To understand the doctrine of predestination correctly we should view it from the standpoint of a Christian who is experiencing and enjoying fellowship with his heavenly Father in the Holy Spirit through the forgiveness in our Lord Jesus Christ. The Bible regularly treats the subject from this point of view. As a Christian reflects on the grace of God which he is experiencing in his own life, he cannot but attribute it all to God's goodness. In himself he knows he deserves nothing. Paul said, "Nothing good dwells in me, that is in my flesh".[40] There is nothing in us of ourselves which deserves God's favour, but only God's condemnation,[41] and yet how wonderfully Christians experience this favour, for the Christian life is one of peace with God through forgiveness, joy in his presence and love towards him and others by his Spirit, faith in daily life and sure hope for the future, a daily fellowship with God through prayer and his Word. This relationship to God is God's gift, and it springs entirely from God's initiative. Jesus said to his disciples, "You did not choose me, but I chose you".[42] Our present Christian experience and our future hope are attributed in the Bible to God's decision, a decision which was made from the beginning of creation with regard

40 Rom 7:18
41 Rom 5:18
42 John 15:16

to us personally: "God has chosen you from the beginning for salvation through sanctification by the Spirit and faith in the truth";[43] and "God has not destined us for wrath, but for obtaining salvation through our Lord Jesus Christ".[44] Speaking of Christians, Paul said that they are "vessels of mercy, which he prepared beforehand for glory".[45] As we experience our Christian status as adopted sons of God, all the glory and the thankfulness of this state of things must be given to God. It is not shared partly with ourselves, as though we had contributed the vital link which made the difference between death and life.

God's sovereignty in salvation

The clearest illustration of God's sovereignty in salvation is the life of the apostle Paul. He was a man totally immersed in his prejudices. On his own initiative, he had asked for authority to journey to Damascus to arrest and imprison believers.[46] He certainly did not seem a bright prospect for conversion, nor was he. His conversion resulted from an extraordinary intervention by God on his behalf. He was converted because as the risen Lord himself put it, he was "a chosen instrument".[47] A light shone around him and he heard the voice of Jesus addressing him. Indeed the heavens were opened and he had a vision of our Lord so bright that he was blinded. It is not surprising that after such an experience he should recognize Jesus as Lord and give his

43 2 Thess 2:13
44 1 Thess 5:9
45 Rom 9:23
46 Acts 9:1-2
47 Acts 9:15

life to his service. It is plain that his conversion is to be attributed entirely to God. It took extraordinary means to bring this 'chosen instrument' into the kingdom. The same is true of the conversion of everyone, though normally it is not so spectacular. The initiative lies entirely with God. It must be so because in ourselves we are blind and cannot see the truth.[48] The mind of the flesh is at enmity against God and is not subject to God's will, nor indeed can it be.[49] God must intervene. He alone can open the eyes of the spiritually blind,[50] take away the stony heart,[51] and re-create the personal relationship with himself. For when a man is in Christ, said Paul, "he is a new creation",[52] and it is God the Creator to whom alone this new creation is to be attributed.

The doctrine of predestination is another way of saying that God is sovereign in salvation; it is he who chooses those whom he adopts as sons.[53] It is he who re-creates them from dead sinners to living saints. Even our response of faith is God's gift, given according to his purpose. Thus Paul told the Philippians that it was God's gift to them that they believed on Jesus.[54] Frequently in the Bible, repentance is said to be the gift of God,[55] and this is natural because we have not the power of self-recovery within ourselves to turn back from a self-centred life to a God-centred life. If anyone repents in

48 2 Cor 4:4
49 Rom 8:7
50 2 Cor 4:4-6
51 Ezek 36:26
52 2 Cor 5:17
53 Eph 1:5
54 Phil 1:29; cf. Eph 2:8-9
55 Acts 5:31, 11:18; 2 Tim 2:25

this radical way, it is God's gift to him. Christians know this to be the case. As they reflect on their own experience, they recognize that were it not for the grace of God they would still be living the old life of self-centredness and sin.

Predestination is full of comfort

Belief in the doctrine of predestination does not come naturally; it is only because it is so clearly taught in Scripture that anyone holds it, and yet when it is firmly grasped it has a tremendous effect in releasing our spirits from anxiety and stress. The evangelist who knows that God is sovereign in salvation does not feel driven to all sorts of expedients to get people converted. He rests in confidence in God. He will rely primarily on prayer and on preaching the clear truth of the gospel in the context of love and relationship, because he knows that the word of the cross is the power of God to salvation.[56] He will not be driven to obtain decisions by methods and expedients which may be unworthy of that gospel with which he has been entrusted, for he knows that it is God who gives repentance and faith in fulfilling his purposes of grace and salvation. Not that belief in God's sovereignty in salvation will excuse lethargy in prayer or slackness in preparation on the part of the minister or individual Christian, or sitting back with the pretext that God will save those whom he has predestined, for God works his purposes of grace through us and through our natures and our gifts, and we must be obedient in the use of our gifts and opportunities, for we are responsible and will have to

56 1 Cor 1:18

give an account before the judgement seat of God.[57]

There is a two-sidedness which cannot be escaped. God is sovereign in salvation; we are responsible in our obedience. The writer of Acts found no contradiction here. In Acts 13:48, he described the results of the preaching of Paul and Barnabas in terms of God's sovereignty: "As many as had been appointed to eternal life believed". A few verses later in 14:1 he put the other side, attributing the result to the fervency of the preachers: "[The apostles] spoke in such a manner that a great multitude believed". Both are true at the same time; God is sovereign—we are responsible. Those who believe and receive salvation, reconciliation, adoption and the Spirit's presence, and are made inheritors of God's kingdom are to understand that their decision for Christ was God's gift in accordance with his purpose, determined on before creation began. Paul said we are "vessels of mercy, which he prepared beforehand for glory".[58] The destinations of the lost and the saved are separated more widely than any gulf imaginable.[59] It would be intolerable if our being on the blessed side of this awful distinction were to be attributed to some virtue in ourselves, some cleverness, some response initiating within ourselves. It would be monstrous if we were to attribute to ourselves the fact that we have received the unspeakable blessings of being the inheritors of God's kingdom,[60] of having his name on our foreheads, of seeing his face and dwelling in his presence for ever.[61] And yet this

57 1 Cor 4:1-5
58 Rom 9:23
59 Luke 16:26
60 Matt 25:34
61 Rev 22:3-5

would be the case if our salvation depended in any way at all upon our own decision apart from God's prior decision. Only the doctrine of predestination prevents us from being engulfed in such an impious doctrine as to attribute the difference between ourselves in heaven and those lost in hell to some response or decision that we ourselves contributed. Of ourselves, we are all the same, lost through our own deserts. The difference between those who are lost and those who are being saved rests in God's decision made before the world was. God is righteous, God is wise and God is loving, and he has mercy on whom he will.[62]

Unbelief

As the preacher contemplates the great number of people who reject the message of God's grace which he has delivered in God's name, he cannot help but weep over them as Christ wept over Jerusalem. Yet it is interesting to note that the ultimate explanation that the Scriptures offer for this unbelief is the predestination of God. Thus Peter said that "they stumble because they are disobedient to the word, and to this doom they were also appointed".[63] As John contemplated the ineffectiveness of Jesus' ministry in drawing the Jewish people to himself, he rested in the predestinating purposes of God, made known long before through the prophet Isaiah: "Who has believed our message? And to whom has the arm of Yahweh been revealed?"[64] "For this cause", John went on to say, "they could not believe,

62 Rom 9:18
63 1 Pet 2:8
64 Isaiah 53:1, quoted at John 12:38.

for Isaiah said again, 'He has blinded their eyes, and he hardened their heart; lest they see with their eyes, and perceive with their heart, and be converted, and I heal them'. These things Isaiah said, because he saw his glory, and he spoke of him."[65] In this John was following and echoing the thoughts of his Master. For when Jesus was reflecting on the rejection of the gospel by Capernaum and Bethsaida and Chorazin, he prayed, "I praise you, O Father, Lord of heaven and earth, that you hid these things from the wise and intelligent… Yes, Father, for thus it was well-pleasing in your sight".[66] Again when Jesus was confronted with the impenitent unbelief of his Jewish hearers he found the explanation of this extraordinary phenomenon, that the people of God should reject the Word of God delivered by the Son of God, in the predestination of God. "You do not believe", he told his hearers, "because you are not of my sheep. My sheep hear my voice";[67] and again, "For this reason you do not hear them, because you are not of God".[68] He also said, "No one can come to me, unless the Father who sent me draws him";[69] and "No one can come unto me, unless it has been granted him from the Father";[70] and "All that the Father gives me shall come to me".[71] When John reviewed the ministry of Jesus, he attributed to the predestination of God its failure to evoke faith. When Paul faced the same extraordinary fact that the people of God

65 John 12:38-41, quoting Isaiah 6:10.
66 Matt 11:25-26
67 John 10:26-27
68 John 8:47
69 John 6:44
70 John 6:65
71 John 6:37

rejected the Messiah of God, he too found the explanation in the predestination of God:

> It is not as though the word of God has failed. For they are not all Israel who are descended from Israel… for though the twins were not yet born, and had not done anything good or bad, in order that God's purpose according to his choice might stand, not because of works, but because of him who calls, it was said to her "The older will serve the younger". Just as it is written, "Jacob I loved, but Esau I hated".
>
> What shall we say then? There is no injustice with God, is there? May it never be! For he says to Moses, "I will have mercy on whom I have mercy, and I will have compassion on whom I have compassion". So then it depends not on the man who wills or the man who runs, but on God who has mercy.[72]

The unbelief of his hearers should fill the preacher's eyes with tears and his heart with yearning, as it did for Jesus and Paul, but the preacher knows that the unbelief of the hearer of the gospel is not outside God's predestinating purposes. In this way it will not discourage him nor make him relax his efforts to fulfil the commission to preach the gospel to the whole creation; but the knowledge of God's predestination will relieve him of tension; it will help him to escape unworthy methods and to avoid psychologically damaging introspection. He will know himself to be the Lord's servant and messenger gathering the Lord's people, that is, Christ's elect, according to God's eternal purposes[73]—

72 Rom 9:6-16
73 Acts 18:10; Matt 24:31

purposes which the Scriptures reveal to be of infinite and overwhelming blessing to the world.

The golden chain of blessing

Because the Bible so clearly teaches the doctrine of predestination, Christians ought to embrace it without hesitation, for it is certainly true and we should adjust our attitudes in conformity with it. There is a wonderful passage in Romans 8:28-30:

> And we know that God causes all things to work together for good to those who love God, to those who are called according to his purpose. For whom he foreknew, he also predestined to become conformed to the image of his son, that he might be the first-born among many brethren; and whom he predestined, these he also called; and whom he called, these he also justified; and whom he justified, these he also glorified.

Notice the emphasis on God's purpose, which he is fulfilling in our lives that we might be conformed to Christ's likeness. Notice the golden chain "whom he predestined, these he also called; and whom he called, these he also justified; and whom he justified, these he also glorified". None is missing; no link is broken; all attain glory. Those whom he had predestined in due course he called, justified and finally glorified by conforming them to the image of Jesus. It is the work of God. Thanks be to God!

The doctrine reminds us that it is God's purpose to confer blessing. The Scriptures tell us that God chose Abraham in order that he might bless him,[74] and Paul began his letter to

74 Gen 12:1-3

the Ephesians with: "Blessed be the God… who has blessed us with every spiritual blessing… he chose us in [Christ] before the foundation of the world… He predestined us to adoption as sons". The realization of this goodness of God, totally undeserved by us, should make us humble and cause us to appreciate our blessings.

Predestination not based on pre-vision

In considering the doctrine of predestination we must exclude from our thoughts any concept that God's predestination is based on his foresight of our response, or of our virtues or our faith. God's choice was based entirely on his own character. Moses made clear that God's choice of the Israelites was not based on anything within themselves: "Yahweh did not set his love on you, nor choose you because you were more in number than any of the peoples, for you were the fewest of all peoples, but because Yahweh loved you".[75] Our salvation is the result of God's mercy, and mercy is always unmerited.

In Romans 9, Paul unravelled the problem that although Jesus the Messiah had come to God's people, the majority of the Israelites had rejected him. It was a very depressing problem for Paul. He wrote, "I have great sorrow and unceasing grief in my heart. For I could wish that I myself were accursed, separated from Christ for the sake of my brethren, my kinsmen according to the flesh, who are Israelites."[76] In spite of all their privileges, the majority of the Jews were rejecting the Messiah. How was it to be

75 Deut 7:7
76 Rom 9:2-3

explained? Paul attributed it simply to the choice of God. God was having mercy on whom he was having mercy.[77] It has always been so, and at that time also there was a remnant according to election and "the rest were hardened, just as it is written, 'God gave them a spirit of stupor, eyes to see not and ears to hear not'".[78]

We must remember that we have no claims on God. In the first place we were created by him. Can the pot dictate to the potter?[79] There is no unrighteousness in God; all his ways are perfect.[80] We cannot probe the purposes of God beyond what he has revealed to us in Scripture. We know his character of love and graciousness, of wisdom and righteousness. He is dealing with a sinful and rebellious race, creatures who reject their Creator, yet he has mercy; and his actions of salvation spring from within his character of wisdom and love and righteousness. God chooses. Of Abraham's children it was Isaac whom God chose, and of Isaac's two children, who were twins and so absolutely equal, Jacob was chosen, not Esau the elder.

Paul is aware of the intellectual problem posed by God's sovereign discrimination, but he does not answer it in any simple manner. He imagines an objector saying that God's choice of one rather than another is unjust, but Paul will not allow any thought that God could be unjust. God, who is the source of our sense of justice, will not contradict what is just by any of his actions. But God is free in choosing on whom he will have mercy. Mercy springs entirely from within the

77 Rom 9:18
78 Rom 11:8
79 Isa 29:16; cf. Rom 9:20-21
80 Deut 32:4

one who is merciful. No rebellious sinner (as we all are) can *demand* that God should be merciful on him or on anyone else. But God has mercy on whom he will, and whom he will he hardens.

Once again the apostle imagines an objector saying that this is unfair. The apostle replies:

> On the contrary, who are you, O man, who answers back to God… What if God, although willing to demonstrate his wrath and to make his power known, endured with much patience vessels of wrath prepared for destruction? And he did so in order that he might make known the riches of his glory upon vessels of mercy, which he prepared beforehand for glory, even us, whom he also called…[81]

Paul recognized the problems of the doctrine of predestination, but he did not take the easy way out, and say that God's decisions are based on his foresight of our response, for this is not true. On the contrary, our response, our reaction, is based on God's foreordination, and his decisions are based only on himself, on his goodness and mercy, on his wisdom and his will. We must not allow ourselves to adopt a solution of which Paul knows nothing as he grapples with this problem of predestination. Yet God's hardening of the sinner is not apart from the sinner's hardening of his own heart. "He hardens whom he desires", said Paul,[82] but on the other hand the Scripture addresses a word to us: "Do not harden your hearts".[83] Of Pharaoh,

81 Rom 9:20-24
82 Rom 9:18b
83 Ps 95:8

the Bible says both that God hardened his heart and that Pharaoh hardened his heart, for both are true at the same time.[84] Pharaoh's will is within the sovereign will of God. Pharaoh wanted to harden his heart, he willed to harden his heart, and God willed that Pharaoh should harden his heart, so that from this sin of Pharaoh God should bring salvation to the world.

We sinners have no right to be angry with God because of the way things happen. We all deserve God's judgement, and if we are not experiencing that judgement to the full immediately, that is due to God's long-suffering. Sinners have no claims on God, no right to be angry with God, for we all deserve a great deal more than anything that might be happening to us at present. If we receive any blessings, and especially if we receive restoration of fellowship through salvation in Christ, it is because of God's mercy.

Immediately after our Lord had reflected on the mystery of God's predestination with regard to the blindness of the townspeople of Capernaum with the words "I praise you, Father... for thus it was well-pleasing in your sight", he repeated the gracious invitation of the gospel: "Come to me, all who are weary and heavy laden, and I will give you rest".[85] There are always these two sides of the truth to be kept in mind at the same time. On the one hand, there is God's sovereignty, having mercy on those who could not possibly be saved apart from his mercy; and on the other, our responsibility to respond and to believe the gospel. Paul kept both sides of the truth before his readers in Romans

84 Exod 7:3, 22; 8:15
85 Matt 11:25-28

9-11. In chapter 9, he emphasized God's sovereignty in predestination and election, but he completed his discussion of this subject in chapter 11 by reminding his readers that those who are lost are lost through their own unbelief, while if his readers hope to be saved it can only be by their continuing in faith. Otherwise, they too will be lost like the rest.

Yet we must not jump to the conclusion that this faith originates in ourselves. It is our faith, it is true, but it is God's gift to us. And because it is God's gift to us we may look to the future with confidence that he will continue to give us the grace to believe. As Hebrews puts it, Christ will save to the very end those who come to God by him.[86] If we are Christ's sheep, none can pluck us out of his hand.[87] Our confidence for the future (and we should all have this confidence) rests in God, not in ourselves, for God has promised to be faithful and to complete that which he has begun in us.[88]

Assurance of future salvation is sometimes said to be presumption. It is anathematized by the Council of Trent for this reason.[89] But it is a question of the ground on which this assurance rests. If it rests on our good works, it would indeed be presumptuous of us to assume that these are good enough to merit salvation or that we will have the strength to persevere. But if our assurance rests on a knowledge of God's promises and his faithfulness, it is not presumption but an act of true faith. Such assurance should be possessed by every believer. So long as the child of God is looking into the face of God, assurance is God-honouring. But to

86 Heb 7:25
87 John 10:27-28
88 1 Thess 5:23-24; Phil 1:6
89 Council of Trent, session 6, chapter 9 and canon 16, 1547.

look away from God and to base assurance on something in ourselves, and not solely on God's grace and promises, is indeed irreligious presumption. Yet it is God's will that every child of his should have assurance of his perseverance and future salvation. One of the objects of John's First Epistle is that his readers might possess this full assurance, for without it Christian joy is diminished and fellowship with God defective.[90]

It is a very important aspect of the doctrine of predestination that God will be faithful and that we may rest in this faithfulness. He will keep his promise, for he is faithful and will do it.[91] If our salvation were to depend on ourselves it would be presumptuous for us to be sure that our future will be in heaven. But since salvation is entirely God's gift from beginning to end, we may rest in thankfulness on his faithfulness, that he will complete the salvation of those whom he chose before the foundation of the world. And we may accept with equanimity, indeed with joy, the events which his goodness allows to enter our lives, knowing that all things work together for good to those that love God, to them who are called according to his purpose. For those whom he called, them also he predestined to be conformed to the image of his Son. We may work in his service without the tension of thinking that everything depends on ourselves, and we may trust him for the future, knowing that those whom he foreknew he also called, and those whom he called he also justified and those whom he justified he also glorified. For God has not appointed us to

90 1 John 1:3-4, 2:26-27, 3:18-20, 5:13
91 1 Thess 5:23-24; 1 Cor 1:8-9

wrath but to the attaining of salvation through our Lord Jesus Christ.[92] We should put an inestimable value on our inheritance.[93]

Paul completed his discussion of the doctrine of predestination in Romans 9, 10 and 11 by reminding his readers of the wisdom of God manifested in the extraordinary and unexpected event that, through the rejection of the Messiah by the people of God, the Gentiles are blessed, and in turn through God's work among the Gentiles, the Jews themselves will be converted. He apostrophizes the wisdom and knowledge of God, who has shut up all unto disobedience, that he might have mercy on all. God's wisdom is not fully revealed to us. We do not understand all that lies behind God's purposes in predestination, but we may rest in his wonderful wisdom and believe that the future will be more full of blessing for the whole world than even the present is.

For those who have been chosen by God to be his sons and daughters, not only should there be profound thankfulness to God for his mercy, but a very deep sense of responsibility. We have been chosen that we might become like Jesus in character. This is God's purpose for us and we should make this the chief object of our life, to conform ourselves to the image of his Son. What a glorious purpose God has for us! We have been chosen to set forth God's praise, that we might be to the praise of the glory of his grace.[94] Our lives should be such that God's glory is seen and praised.[95]

92 1 Thess 5:9
93 1 Pet 1:3-5
94 Eph 1:6
95 Matt 5:16

We have been chosen to be blessed and to be a blessing, that through our lives and our words we might bless others with the knowledge of Christ. The privilege is great and the responsibility real.

appendix A

The religions of the world as a source of knowledge of God

Since humanity universally believes that deity is personal and since persons and, *a fortiori*, a personal God are only known in as far as they reveal themselves, the question arises where (if indeed anywhere) deity has revealed itself to mankind. We have seen in chapter 1 that the Bible states that God has revealed himself through the centuries by personally addressing men and women whom he has chosen to receive these communications and his fellowship. This revelation culminated in the presence of Jesus of Nazareth in Palestine in the first century. The Bible further states that this revelation has been inscripturated by God so that the revelation and fellowship are also fully available to us. But has the self-revelation of God been confined to the Christian religion? To extend the concept of revelation to all the religions of the world is a natural answer and it has been given classic expression in *The Constitution of the Church, Lumen Gentium*, one of the official pronouncements of the Second Vatican Council of the Roman Catholic Church. In paragraph 16, the Second Vatican Council affirmed, "The plan of salvation also includes those who acknowledge the Creator. In the first place among these are the Moslems who, professing to hold the faith of Abraham along with us, adore the one and merciful God who in the last day will judge mankind. Nor is God far distant from those who in shadows and images seek the unknown God, for it is he who gives all men life and breath and all things and, as Saviour, wills that all men be saved". The view expressed in this document is very widespread. It was given expression at the Anglican Congress in Toronto in 1963 when the secretary of an important missionary society challenged his hearers to flex "the muscles of our imagination far enough to recognize God's presence in the cave outside Mecca, under the Bo tree and at other points in man's religious pilgrimage".[1]

No revelation in the ethnic religions

However, the knowledge of deity that may be gained by examining the religious notions of humanity, whether Muslims or idolaters, does not extend beyond the knowledge of the existence of a superhuman, powerful, knowledgeable, personal, everlasting being to whom we are related. The religions of the nations do not give a knowledge of the character of God, for the notions of deity in those religions are so diverse that they cancel one another out. We may conclude that although mankind believes in the existence of personal deity it has no personal relationship with deity because it has no consistent or universally held view of the character of deity, which would not be the case if men were in fact related to the same deity through the multiplicity of human religions.

This conclusion is also the view of the Bible. The worshippers of the religions of the world are regarded by the Bible as being ignorant of the true God. When Paul was

1 *Report of Anglican Congress 1963*, SPCK, London, 1963, p. 21.

walking through the market-place at Athens he noticed that it was full of altars to the various deities of the Athenian pantheon. The one that he chose as closest to reality was the altar inscribed "to the unknown God", and taking this inscription as his starting-point, he told the Athenians, "What you worship in ignorance, this I set forth to you".[2]

For Paul, the nations are "without God".[3] They are ignorant of God. "The Gentiles walk", he said, "in the vanity [that is, emptiness] of their mind, being darkened in their understanding, alienated from the life of God because of the ignorance that is in them, because of the hardening of their heart".[4]

This last phrase "the hardening of their heart" points to the reason why the ethnic religions are not in touch with the true God. The religion of the nations is the consequence of the hardening of their heart. Ethnic religions are the result of turning away from God; they are not a feeling after him in order to find him. Such feeling after God to find him is always open to mankind, for he is not far from any of us.[5] But it is a possibility that is not taken. This is plain from Paul's argument in Romans 1. There the apostle makes clear that the religions of the world are the result of rebellion against the true knowledge of God given to man in creation. For through the things that have been made, it is possible to perceive God's everlasting power and divinity, but instead of responding to that knowledge in the way that our consciences tell us we should, namely by glorifying God

2 Acts 17:23
3 Eph 2:12
4 Eph 4:18
5 Acts 17:27

and giving him thanks for all the benefits that creation has brought us and in this way coming to know God, mankind has refused to have a knowledge of God and has become vain in its reasoning and its ignorant heart has become darkened. Mankind has refused to respond to God known in creation, it has refused to give him the glory due to him and the thanks for benefits received through his benefaction. Men have turned their back on God, hardened their heart against him and have developed false religions to be a substitute for the true God whom we have refused to acknowledge in the way that we know God should be acknowledged, that is, by thankfulness and praise. The religion of rebels does not yield a knowledge of the true God.

The religions of rebels contain no knowledge of God or relationship with him

The religions of the world are the creation of rebellious men as a substitute for worshipping the true God. Universally mankind has made and worshipped idols as a substitute for acknowledging the true God—a substitute which on analysis is absurd, namely, idols of mortal men, of birds, of animals and of reptiles, as though these were ultimate reality. Truly "their senseless heart has been darkened".[6] There is therefore no knowledge of the true God to be found in the worshipping that goes on in connection with the religions of the nations. It is not there that we can seek for knowledge of God. The Bible is quite clear on this. The Old Testament constantly describes the religions of the

6 Rom 1:21

nations around Israel as emptiness, vanity. The idols, their gods, are nonentities. It is not to be expected therefore that knowledge of the true God is to be found by examining the religion and worship of nonentities.

There is a further and perhaps more compulsive reason still for rejecting the study of religion as a way which leads to the truth about divine things, for the idols of the nations, in themselves nonentities and the result of God giving men up to their disobedience, become the opportunity by which the evil spirits of the demonic world obtain a control over the minds, hearts and lives of those who worship idols. Paul says in 1 Corinthians 10:20, "The things which the Gentiles sacrifice, they sacrifice to devils, and not to God", and this is fully in keeping with the repeated testimony of the Old Testament with regard to the idolatry which the children of Israel fell into from time to time. For example, in the song of Moses, "They sacrificed unto demons which were no God, to gods whom they knew not, to new gods that came up of late, whom your fathers dreaded not",[7] or again in Psalm 106:37, "They sacrificed their sons and their daughters unto demons". In Revelation 9:20 the worship of the religions of the world is said to be the worship of devils.

The conclusion is clear that in the ethnic religions, both of the ancient world as well as of our modern times, there is no knowledge of God to be found. The worshippers of those religions are not in fellowship with God; they are not related to God through their religious worship. They open themselves up to the influence of demons and are in fact worshipping evil spirits under the veil of their idols, so

7 Deut 32:17

that we may conclude that their notions of deity are devil-inspired. This biblical teaching is very different from that of modern theological thought, reflected for example in the trend in universities to substitute the study of religions for the study of Christian theology.

The New Testament constantly warns Christians to have nothing at all to do with idolatry. John concluded his letter with the words: "My little children, guard yourselves from idols" and Paul in several places warned his converts that idolaters will not inherit the kingdom of God, but on the contrary the wrath of God will overtake those who follow this form of religion.[8] In New Testament times there was no other form of religion among the nations except idolatry, so in condemning idolatry the New Testament condemns all the religions of the nations and the terms of its condemnation are the severest possible. If the New Testament is to be normative for our thinking about God and where he may be found, we must not yield to the temptation of seeking him in the thought structures created by the ethnic religions which even today are essentially idolatrous. This exclusivism is very unpleasant to the modern mind but it expresses the New Testament emphasis which is fully in keeping with that of the Old. Israel was to have nothing whatever to do with the religions of the nations for there was no truth to be found in them.

Ethnic religions are not seeking God

There is nothing in the world or in God's relation to it which prevents us from finding God in the world. Nor has God

8 1 Cor 6:9; Eph 5:5

left himself without witness, in that he did good, giving us rain and fruitful seasons, filling our hearts with food and gladness. The fault is in ourselves if we do not perceive this witness. For the god of this world blinds the eyes of the unbelieving. Even those whom the apostle was addressing as he reminded them of this witness were at that very moment engaged in idolatry.[9] They were ignoring the witness. God has promised that those who seek him will find him. He will respond to those who with a true heart seek him, because he is not far from any of us. But the Bible teaches that "there are none who seek after God. They have all turned aside."[10] Instead of seeking God we turn our backs on him; instead of making the right response we refuse that response. We refuse to have knowledge of the truth and make a false god in its place. The consequence is that our relationship with God is cut. There is no knowledge of God in our lives and the religions of the world which we create in the place of the true God are not a means for knowing him or a way by which we may relate ourselves to him. It is true that there remains much that is noble in human nature and in human relationships, through the grace and long-suffering of God, but this genuineness in human relationships, man with man, should not be mistaken for knowledge of God. Knowledge of God and relationship with him has perished through sin.

To sum up, the Bible states that human religion is the result of rebellion against God, and no knowledge of God is in it. Because they would not have God in their mind, the nations created for themselves idols which on a moment's

9 Acts 14:18
10 Rom 3:11-12

reflection should have been seen to be the most ridiculous form of god. Secondly, the Bible says that the idols and gods of the nations are empty, vanity, nonentities. Nothing corresponds to them in reality, therefore it is plain that no knowledge of God can be found from the philosophy and the reasoning that surrounds these religions. Thirdly, the Bible says that the religions of the world are directed towards the demon world. It is as though the vacuum caused through turning away from the true God is filled by evil spirits from the spiritual world that is in rebellion against him. Fourthly, the Bible is clear that there is absolute ignorance of God in the religions of the world. For these reasons it is plain that a knowledge of God, that is to say, a relationship with the true personal God, is not to be arrived at through these religions. Religious studies will help the student understand human nature and human culture but will not contribute to his understanding of God. Anthropology is important, but it is not theology.

appendix B

The implications of the doctrine of the Trinity for theology and for ordinary life

The Trinity and theology

The Trinity, God himself, is an awesome subject. God is the high and lofty one who inhabits eternity, whose name is holy. He dwells in the high and holy place, but also with those of a contrite and humble spirit, to revive the spirit of the humble and to revive the heart of the contrite ones.[1]

Because of the humility of God in dwelling with us and speaking to us, we may speak to him and speak of him to one another.

The doctrine of the Trinity is the glory of the Christian faith. It is drawn entirely from revelation. It depends on the absolute truth of the sentences through which the Scriptures teach us about God and his nature, his character, his purposes, his actions and promises. The doctrine depends, for example, on the infallibility and inerrancy of the teaching in St John's Gospel, or the Epistle to the Ephesians or the last paragraph of St Matthew's Gospel, because the doctrine of the Trinity is not enunciated fully in any one passage but is gathered from many statements of

1 Isa 57:15

the Scriptures. If we cannot rely on the verbal inspiration of Scripture, the doctrine of the Trinity has no basis.

The teaching of Scripture about the trinitarian nature of God is succinctly summarized in articles one, two and five of the Thirty-nine Articles of the Church of England. But its classical statement is in the Athanasian Creed. This creed is regarded with disfavour by some people at present, especially its opening and closing statements that the Christian faith is "we worship one God in Trinity and Trinity in unity; neither confounding the persons nor dividing the substance", and that unless a person holds this faith he cannot be saved. However, the truth of the creed is confirmed by Peter's words that Jesus is "the head of the corner and in none other is there salvation"[2] and that "whoever calls upon the name of the Lord shall be saved".[3]

For it is not possible to hold the unity of God and to call on Jesus as Lord unless you believe the doctrine of the Trinity.

The doctrine of the Trinity was believed by the Christian church from the beginning, for from the beginning believers acknowledged Jesus as their Lord and their God and prayed to him, though he had prayed to the Father. Yet they remained orthodox Jews, saying in their devotions twice a day, "Hear, O Israel, the Lord is our God, the Lord is one Lord".[4]

Josephus ascribes the command to say the shema twice daily to Moses.[5] The Mishnah takes the saying of the shema twice daily for granted.[6]

2 Acts 4:11-12
3 Acts 2:21; cf. Paul in Acts 16:31 and Romans 10:13.
4 Deut 6:4
5 *Antiquities* 4.7
6 *Beracot* 1.1-2

In fact, if it had not been recorded in Matthew 28:19 that Jesus taught the disciples the doctrine of the Trinity, we would have to postulate that he had done so. These words of Jesus in Matthew 28:19 encapsulate the doctrine of the Trinity. The name of the Lord remains one name, yet now God is to be known as Father, Son and Holy Spirit—distinct, personal and equal.

The fact that God is Trinity shows that personal relationship is basic reality, that is, that:

(i) There is nothing more ultimate than personal relationship. Being, considered in itself, is an abstraction. Ultimate, true and real being is and always has been being-in-personal-relationship.

(ii) It follows that metaphysics of the Absolute or a theology of an impersonal God, such as Aristotle's, and any theology of Being which is not thought of as being-in-relationship has an error at its centre.

(iii) It follows that the subject matter of theology is not God, but God in his relationship, for the essence of God is in eternal relationship. Relationship with God and with one another is the subject matter of Scripture. It teaches the infallible truth inerrantly on these matters. God is Trinity eternally. The first words of the Bible are "In the beginning God created the heaven and the earth", that is, revelation begins with a statement of God in relationship with our environment and ourselves.

The Trinity and personal relationships

1. Other-person-centredness

Personal relationship is ultimate reality. The basic requirement for the establishment and maintenance of true personal relationship is *other-person-centredness*, that is, genuine interest in the other person and his welfare and the forwarding of that welfare by every appropriate means at one's disposal. This means that absolute other-person-centredness is the most real thing in being a person.

There can be no trace of self-centredness in true personal relationship. The smallest degree of self-centredness diminishes the relationship. Complete self-centredness is the negation of any personal relationship. The complete absence of relationship between persons is hell.

Since God is *actus purus* (i.e. there is no mere potentiality in him), his other-person-centredness is complete, and active in conferring benefits on the other person all the time.

Thus we read that in the Trinity the Father always gives the Son everything:

> ...as the Father has life in himself, even so he gave to the Son to have life in himself.[7]
>
> The Father loves the Son and has given all things into his hand.[8]
>
> The Father loves the Son and shows him all things that he does.[9]

Similarly of the Son we read of his true personal response to the initiatives of the Father:

> I seek not my own will, but the will of him that sent me.[10]

The Son's response springs from his other-person-centredness:

7 John 5:26
8 John 3:35
9 John 5:20
10 John 5:30

> I love the Father and as the Father gave me commandment, even so I do.[11]
>
> The Son does nothing of himself but as the Father taught him.[12]

The Spirit, too, is other-person-centred within the Trinity:

> He shall not speak from himself; but whatsoever things he shall hear, these shall he speak.[13]

He does not glorify himself but glorifies the Son, just as the Son does not seek his own glory but the Father's. In the Trinity there is complete mutual other-person-centredness, as:

> All things that are mine are thine and thine are mine… All things whatsoever the Father has are mine.[14]

This complete other-person-centredness and mutual self-giving one to the other makes personal knowledge of each other possible. Thus:

> The Father knows me and I know the Father.[15]
>
> No-one knows the Son except the Father and no-one knows the Father except the Son and he to whom the Son wills to reveal him.[16]
>
> You shall know that I am in my Father, and you in me and I in you.[17]

11 John 14:31
12 John 8:28
13 John 16:13
14 John 17:10, 16:15
15 John 10:15
16 Matt 11:27
17 John 14:20

Other-person-centredness is activity; it is not merely benevolence but beneficence.

It is more usually described by the Hebrew word *chesed*, the Greek *agape*, the Latin *caritas*, and the English *love*, all of which are terms for other-person-centredness in attitude and action.

God's centre of his activity is in the welfare of the other. It is not confined to the relations between the persons of the Trinity, but being basic to his nature of relationship extends to his creation. Thus:

> The Lord is good to all and his tender mercies are over all that he has made.[18]
>
> He makes his sun to rise on the evil and the good and sends rain on the just and the unjust.[19]
>
> He is kind to the unthankful and evil.[20]

This absolute other-person-centredness, which is the inalienable element in perfect, personal relationship, as in the Trinity, is the ground of our salvation.

> God commended his own love toward us, in that while we were yet sinners, Christ died for us.[21]
>
> God so loved the world that he gave his only Son.[22]

It is a great assurance to know that God is infinitely concerned with our welfare and with advancing it. His whole infinite being is absolutely and always centred on each of us, and he

18 Ps 145:9
19 Matt 5:45
20 Luke 6:35
21 Rom 5:8
22 John 3:16

is always engaged in advancing our benefit.

The most ultimate thing that can be said of God is that he is Trinity. He always has been, always will be. Three persons in one God, one God in personal relationship within himself.

He has created man in his own image and likeness. This means that man is fundamentally a being in personal relationship, in relationship with God and with his fellows.

Therefore, humanity's nature is created to facilitate personal relationship to God and to one another.

The establishment, maintenance and deepening of personal relationship is the true object for human activity, relationship with God and with fellow men.

Human beings are spirits, created for fellowship with God. Deepening of friendship with God is the object of our spiritual life. Biblical spirituality is friendship with God, that is, growing in knowing God. Jesus calls those who follow him his friends. He shares with them what he has received from the Father.[23] There is a mutual dwelling of us in the Father and the Son, as the Father and the Son indwell us by the Spirit.[24]

Contrast this biblical faith and spirituality with what goes under the name of religion and spirituality.

Religion arises out of ignorance of God as the result of rebellion. Those who refuse to have God in their knowledge, God gives up to religion.[25]

But the Christian faith is friendship with God, knowing

23 John 15:15
24 John 14:23; 17:21, 23, 26
25 Rom 1:18-32

God or, rather, being known by him, indwelling him and he indwelling us, through the Spirit. The Christian faith and the Christian life are firmly trinitarian.

Holiness is knowing God and obeying him as a result of personal relationship with him, through knowing and meditating on his word and consequently being consciously in his presence. This is biblical spirituality.

Humanity was created in the image of God to have fellowship also one with the other. Thus the establishment and deepening of personal relationship between one another is also the true object of human activity.

Since God is in personal relationship within himself it follows that true personal relationship is blissful and is the basis of happiness. This truth is confirmed in human experience. We find that enjoyment is deepened when it is shared.

Men and women are to imitate God in being absolutely other-person-centred, without any trace of self-centredness. That is, they are to be benevolent and beneficent to everybody, in attitude and action, to forward the welfare of others, as their own circumstances and responsibilities allow.

The virtues which are peculiarly Christian virtues spring from this absolute-other-person-centredness. Such virtues are, for example: forgiveness, humility, meekness and long suffering.

In the non-Christian world these characteristics are not regarded as virtues but are seen as weaknesses (cf. Sulla's self composed epitaph).[26] But they are strongly and consistently

26 The Roman general and dictator, whose epitaph read: "No friend ever outstripped me in doing good, no enemy in doing harm".

inculcated in Scripture and are exemplified in the lives of the biblical saints, and pre-eminently in Jesus.

The concept of other-person-centredness controls the content of these virtues. For example, humility is not servility, but a forgetfulness of self in the presence of the other person. Meekness is not weakness and timidity, but the absence of self-assertiveness, the absence of self-centredness. Moses was by no means a weak man, yet he is described as the meekest man in all the earth.[27]

Humility is an essential virtue if other-person-centredness is to be perfect and complete. Humility is the taking of one's thoughts off oneself in order to be mindful of the welfare of the other. In true relationship between persons, neither should be thinking of themselves at the expense of the other.

God is humble. He does not direct attention to himself for his own sake. He is not concerned with status, but he is concerned that others should recognize their relationship to him, for this is their welfare, for this is truth. The ignoring of the truth, or its denial, is always to the disadvantage of those who do this.

God does not blow his own trumpet! He does not bear witness to himself, except when knowledge about the truth, about himself, is to the advantage of the hearer. Thus Jesus does not proclaim his deity, except indirectly, in order that the listener might arrive at this conclusion himself; or in answer to a direct question.

God commands, "Let another man praise you and not

27 Num 12:3

your own mouth, a stranger and not your own lips".[28] Paul follows this injunction. He did not commend himself unless it was for the benefit of his readers.[29]

The clearest expression in Scripture of God's humility is in Isaiah 57:15: "For thus says the high and lofty One who inhabits eternity, whose name is Holy: I dwell in the high and holy place, with him also that is of a contrite and humble spirit, to revive the spirit of the humble and to revive the heart of the contrite ones".

Humility characterized the life of Jesus.[30] He invited the burdened in spirit to learn from him in this respect: "I am meek and lowly in heart". "I am among you as he who serves."[31] This self-testimony was for the purpose of our following him for our good.

Other-person-centredness is only another way of saying love; that is, love in its biblical meaning.

2. Communication

The second essential requirement for personal relationship is personal *communication*. There must be mutual indwelling of person with person through mutual communication of person to person. Thus in the creation narrative we read of God conferring within the Trinity. God said, "Let us make man in our image, after our likeness…"[32] It is entirely appropriate that there should be an intimation of the trinitarian nature of God at this point, for the narrative had

28 Prov 27:2
29 2 Cor 12:19
30 Matt 11:28-29
31 Luke 22:27
32 Gen 1:26

reached the stage of the creation of man "in the image of God", that is to say, a being-in-personal-relationship. This verse is not a proof of the doctrine of the Trinity, but since God is eternally Trinity, as is established from elsewhere in Scripture, and since all Scripture is spoken to us by God,[33] it is perverse not to acknowledge that his trinitarian nature is reflected in the language of revelation at this most appropriate juncture. "God created man in his own image, in the image of God created he him; male and female created he them." No sooner had he created them thus, as personal-beings-in-relationship, as he is personal-being-in-relationship, than he spoke to them communicating his mind and will to them, telling them that he was giving them his own dominion over his creation and that he was providing plenteously for their needs.

Communication is essential for personal relationship. Communication is a mutual activity. One party must speak and the other hear and respond by speaking, which in turn must be heard and responded to. Failure in communication results in the atrophy and death of the relationship.

In our relations with one another we must give ourselves to one another, we must communicate our minds and our feelings by our words to one another, whether through voice, or gesture, or expression, or action. We dare not indulge in the sinful luxury of huffiness. Refusal to communicate weakens and kills personal relationship in which happiness is alone to be found. If we are to have personal relationship with God, God must speak to us, communicating himself to us. We must hear his word and respond by faith, believing

33 2 Tim 3:16

that word, trusting it and obeying it, for to us God is his word. We, in turn, must respond by communing with God, speaking to him in praise and thanks and prayer.

God has created men and women as persons, to be in personal relationship with him and with one another, and to speak to one another, expressing their thoughts, feelings and personality to him and to one another.

The image of God, which is persons in relationship, is built on the attributes of conscious thought, will, feeling, sense of right and wrong and of justice and of judgement, the concept of God and a sense of his existence, the gift of language with similar attributes. On these are built the relationship of friendship and fellowship, and the sharing of a common life through mutual self-giving.

When man broke his fellowship with God through self-will and disobedience, his personal relationship with God and with his fellow man was marred and progressively destroyed. Thus he lost the image of God which is perfect personal relationship, which expresses itself in active other-person-centredness and for which he had been created. In this sense, he irretrievably lost the image of God. He became irreversibly self-centred towards God and towards his fellows. But in another sense he retained it, for he remained a person, created for personal relationship. Thus, after the Fall, man is still said to be in the image of God, and this is the ground on which murder is forbidden[34] for murder is the nadir of personal relationship; no action less other-person-centred can be imagined, nor more out of keeping with the image of God in which we were created.

34 Gen 9:6

It is in Jesus Christ that God's image in man has been restored. He was perfectly other-person-centred, actively supplying our needs, fully trusting and obeying his Father. Through the Spirit of Jesus, those who are in Christ are being transformed into that same image[35] and so the purpose of God in creation is being fulfilled.[36]

In the Garden of Eden, God began personal communion with man but man broke off that relationship by disobedience. Had God accepted the breach there would have been no further need for God to speak to us. But it was his will and purpose to restore the fellowship, and this meant that he continued and continues to speak to mankind. He has done this in a variety of ways but for us today he speaks through Scripture, his written word.

Since humanity's relationships reflect God's relationships, being the image of God, human language, which describes them, is a true vehicle for God to use to communicate his relationship to us. Thus our God-talk is univocal and not analogical. We may know God truly though still dimly, in this life. He has spoken to us, and speaks to us, in the words of Scripture.

God had each of us in mind when he breathed out the words of Scripture. Our mind boggles at the idea that God had each of us in mind when he inspired the written, and therefore unchangeable, words. But God is infinite in knowledge and power. It presents no problem to him. As Paul says, "What was written before time was written for

35 2 Cor 3:18
36 Rom 8:29

our instruction",[37] and "All Scripture has been breathed out by God [i.e. spoken by God] that God's man [i.e. person] might be thoroughly equipped for every good work" (i.e. the Bible is sufficient to guide us in all our relationships).[38]

In this connection Jesus' words to the Sadducees are most interesting. He asked them, "Have you never read what was spoken to you by God?"[39] Notice it is the Scripture that Jesus said was spoken by God. Something we have in our hand, something permanent, and which we can read. But note especially that these words are spoken by God to the present day reader. In Scripture God speaks to us. He communicates with us. Of course it is through the Holy Spirit who indwells us that we hear those words, just as it was through the Holy Spirit that the words were addressed to us in the first place, so many centuries ago.

If the words of Scripture are God's words to us which he is addressing to us in order to communicate himself to us (and this is the clear view of Jesus and the apostles),[40] it follows that what God is saying, what he is communicating to us, is infallible and inerrant. This is axiomatic for the God of Truth. If anything we regard as Scripture is wrong in what it is saying to us about God and ourselves and his will for our relations with him and with one another, that is, about "every good work", or if the Scripture is deceiving us about its own character, then *ipso facto* it is not Scripture, not breathed out by God. It has got into the canon by mistake.

37 Rom 15:4
38 2 Tim 3:16-17
39 Matt 22:31
40 Matt 19:4-5, 22:31; Acts 4:25

The testimony of our Lord and the apostles is to the Scripture, that is, to what we have in our hand, not to the thoughts of the writers, or to their background, but to the propositions they have written and which we may read. It is this word that God is speaking to us. The way to understand what we read is by the historico-grammatical method, not the historico-critical. The study of sources, dates, authorship, is interesting and may be useful for apologetics, but unless it makes clearer the meaning of the written words, unless, that is, it makes clearer what God is saying to us, it is ultimately irrelevant knowledge. But, for the most part, the meaning of Scripture is on the surface, especially if the reader knows the text of the whole of Scripture and in particular the Old Testament as well as the writer did, for Scripture illuminates Scripture, having ultimately only one author, God.

It is important to maintain the view of Scripture which Jesus held and which the apostles held and which the whole Christian church held till recently. Otherwise it is not possible to continue to be a Christian, that is, to have fellowship with God through knowing him, to submit to the lordship of Christ and so be saved, to live the life of faith, and to have a sure and steadfast hope, for it is only through God communicating with us that we can know him personally. Communication is essential for personal relationship.

3. Fairness

A third equally essential element of true personal relationship is *fairness* or righteousness or justice. This consists of treating people according to what they deserve.

Thus constantly we read in Scripture that: God renders

to every man according to their works,[41] and that God is no respecter of persons.[42] Justice is essential for personal relations. Any trace of injustice breaks down the relationship. Thus we read not only "God is love"[43] but first we read "God is light and in him is no darkness at all".[44] God is a righteous God.

In the Trinity, the relationships between the persons are eternally unchanging, but in human life relationships admit of degrees, and the degree of relationship modifies what is deserved.

Thus a rich man who has no relatives would be acting righteously if he left in his will all his estate to be distributed equally to the inhabitants of his village, say $100 to each of the 1,000 inhabitants; but he would not be acting righteously if he were to include wife and children equally with the other inhabitants.

Thus, though on the one hand God's tender mercies are over all his works,[45] yet he works all things together for good to those who love him, to those who are called according to his purpose.[46] His righteousness—that is, his giving to those what they deserve—expresses itself in the salvation of his people. The God-given victories of the people of God over their enemies are "the righteous acts of the Lord".[47] God's righteousness and his salvation of his people are the same.[48]

41 Prov 24:12; Rom 2:6
42 Acts 10:34
43 1 John 4:8
44 1 John 1:5
45 Ps 145:9
46 Rom 8:28
47 1 Sam 12:7
48 Isa 51:5, 56:1

4. Faithfulness

A fourth essential for personal relationship is *faithfulness* (i.e. steadfastness to the relationship).

Faithfulness is not the same as loyalty, in spite of the fact that it is translated by loyalty in some modern English versions of the Bible. Faithfulness is based on truth. Where loyalty does not coincide with faithfulness, it is a vice, and not a virtue.

God is a faithful God. Thus is his description in both Old and New Testaments.[49] He remains true to the relationship he has entered into.

5. Order

Order is the fifth necessity for personal relationship.

Order arises out of differences. There are differences within the Trinity. The Father, the Son, and the Spirit share one essence but are distinct. There are differences among the members of the human race.

The most obvious difference is the difference in sex. Men and women share an identical nature but there are observable differences physically, emotionally and mentally. The differences are not differences in equality, but make men and women distinct. The same is true of individuals. Each is distinct. They are not mere clones.

The distinctions of creation are purposeful, since they are the result of a wise sovereign Creator. They are for the purpose of experiencing and strengthening relationships, of advancing the image of God within us. That is to say, they are for the purpose of serving one another, for this is the

49 Deut 7:9; 1 Pet 4:19

image of God.

Were mankind to be identical clones there would be no need or opportunity of serving one another, for all would have identical resources within themselves. That is to say there would be no possibility of personal relationship through mutual self-giving.

The distinctions within mankind are opportunities for service, that is, for reflecting the character of God who is among us as one who serves.[50]

Order is the structure in which service functions smoothly.

We see order exemplified in the Trinity. The personal relationship within the Trinity is an ordered relationship—Father, Son, Spirit. The essence of order in relationship is that it cannot be reversed without affecting the relationship. Father-Son cannot become Son-Father without changing the relationship.

Relationship implies responsibility, and if this is to be discharged, a priority of responsibility must be recognized in each relationship. That is to say, true personal relationships have a recognized and gladly accepted order within them.

Priority in order implies responsibility for initiating thought and action in line with the principle of other-person-centredness. This priority in responsibility is described in the Bible as headship. Too often we interpret scriptural headship in conformity with headship as exercised in sinful humanity, where it is the equivalent of dominance and the imposition of one's own will on others.

But there is no trace of this in God or in the world as God

50 Luke 22:27

created it. There is headship in the Trinity, accompanied by the response of glad submission and recognition of authority. Divine headship consists of responsibility for initiating benefits evoking the corresponding response of thanks and obedience.

Thus the Father loves the Son and shows him everything he does and the Son acknowledges the Father is greater than the Son.[51] The Father sends the Son.[52] The Father gives him everything.[53] As the Father has life in himself, so he has given the Son to have life in himself.[54]

These relationships between the Father and the Son are eternal relationships. They do not have a beginning. The relationship of Father and Son described as "the Son being in the bosom of the Father"[55] is an eternal relationship. This terminology indicates order in the relationship.

So, too, in the relationship of the Spirit to the Father and the Son, there is order. The Spirit proceeds from the Father[56] and is poured forth on believers by the Son.[57] He is sent by the Father.[58] He is sent by the Son.[59]

This order in the Trinity does not imply inequality, as though, in the modern sense of the words, one is superior and the other inferior, but the order does indicate different functions and responses within the personally related Trinity.

51 John 14:28
52 John 4:34
53 John 13:3
54 John 5:26
55 John 1:18
56 John 15:26
57 Acts 2:33
58 John 14:26
59 John 16:7

God has created the world in accordance with his nature and has created humanity in his image, after his likeness. There is order in the creation and there is order within the personal relationship of humanity. This order within humanity does not imply inequality between the persons but it does indicate that there are different functions and responses to the persons in relationship.

In Scripture God is revealed as head of Christ and Christ as head of the church.[60]

The Father takes the initiative with regard to the Son, showing him everything he does, giving him everything, sharing with him his life-in-himselfness (John 5:19-27).

The Son responds by always doing that which pleases the Father, by always doing and only doing what the Father shows him, by doing always that which the Father commands.

Similarly, in humanity, God has created order. In the same Scripture passage, which teaches that God is the head of Christ and Christ the head of the church, God has revealed that man is the head of woman.[61] This passage controls the meaning of the word "head". Man's headship in relation to woman is of the same character as the headship of God to Christ and of Christ to man, and of Christ to the church. The divine headship which God has conferred on man in the man-woman relationship contains no element in it which is not found in the Father's headship in the Trinity, or Christ's headship in humanity. That is, it is entirely other-person-centred, without so much as

60 1 Cor 11:3; Eph 5:23
61 1 Cor 11:3

a trace of self-centredness. Our Lord affirmed, as we all experience, that in the world headship has been twisted into something quite different. "The kings of the nations have lordship over them... but you shall not be so... I am in the midst of you as he that serves."[62] Headship after the divine pattern is responsibility for taking thought and initiative in forwarding the welfare of those of whom one is head. It consists of nothing else. The responsibility is to further the welfare to the best of one's abilities and circumstances of the other party in the relationship. We all have this responsibility towards others, but in each relationship there is a priority which circumstances or created nature indicates. Authority accompanies the discharging of true responsibility. The response should contain the recognition of this, thanks for the benefit and abiding honour of the one who is giving or has given himself in furtherance of one's welfare.

All men and women have responsibility for one another's welfare according to the changing circumstances of their relationship. It is the relationship which creates the responsibility. In the flux of the circumstances of life, men and women come into many and often changing relationships which carry with them the responsibility of advancing the other's welfare. This responsibility arising from the circumstances of the relationship, carries with it authority for beneficent action. The recipient of the benefit should acknowledge the authority and receive and give thanks for the benefit, and honour the giver.

There are, however, some personal relationships which

62 Luke 22:25-27; cf. Mark 10:42-45

are not the result of changing circumstances in life but are permanent, such as those which result from birth. Our relationship with God and the relationship between men and women partake of this permanent character. The Scriptures make clear that man is the head of woman. Men and women together make up humanity. Men and women are almost 100 per cent the same in physical, emotional and mental make up. Yet there are differences between them, not only physically, which is obvious, but also emotionally and mentally, as careful observation will confirm. These differences do not make one sex better than the other or superior to another, but they further the different responsibilities which belong to the order of their relationship. The differences between masculinity and femininity are part of creation and are consequently purposeful, to enable the responsibilities of the relationship to be perfectly fulfilled.

Sin, which is essentially self-centred, has not only destroyed the personal relationship which man has to God, namely the response of honour, faith, thanks and submission, but has also greatly marred the relationship of men and women. Men have turned headship into self-centred lordship and dominance. They have used their natures, physical, mental and emotional, not to serve but to dominate. Women, too, may use their gifts of nature to dominate.

The re-creation of men and women in Christ does not destroy the order in their relationship but restores it to its divine character in being motivated and directed by love, that is, biblical, divine love of other-person-centredness in attitude and action.

Relationships may change—for example, the parent-child relationship begins at the point of conception, grows to the birth, remains stable through childhood but changes again with growing maturity, and may reverse itself in old age. Each stage in the relationship means a change in the responsibility and thus of the authority inherent in it. But the obligation of honour does not evaporate when the responsibility ceases.

So, too, in the *ad hoc* relationship of daily living and secular life. Circumstances may create a relationship and hence the responsibility for caring for the other's welfare, and changing circumstances may reverse the relationship and hence the responsibility and its consequent authority.

Relationship within the Trinity is unchanging and immutable, and so the order of Father, Son, Spirit remains stable.

But many relationships in modern society are flexible and so responsibility for the other person's welfare is flexible and is determined by the flux of circumstances.

However, there are some human relations that are more stable than this, being based on human nature as God has created it.

These include the relationship of men and women as such. But even in this, it is possible to imagine unusual situations where the normal order of responsibility is affected by the circumstances.

But only those involved in such circumstances can determine what those circumstances require. Thus in the congregation, only the congregation can determine who should lead it in the circumstances they find themselves in.

Absolute ordinations are condemned by the sixth canon

of Chalcedon.[63] Yet these days all ordinations are absolute. If this were remedied, so that only those are ordained who are recognized as ministering to a congregation as their ministers, and they remained ordained only so long as they minister acceptably in that congregation unless they are called and recognized by another congregation, then it would be possible for women to be ordained, at least in theory, for in practice it would not be often (perhaps never) that a spiritual, Bible-instructed congregation concluded that the circumstances it found itself in meant that it should recognize a woman as its teacher and chief minister.

The sin in the Garden of Eden involved a reversal of the created order of relationship. Instead of God, man, woman, animal, the priority became animal (the serpent), woman, man and God, and his word was excluded altogether.

After the Fall, God re-established the order, but now, because of sin, it would be accompanied by pain.

God is ultimate reality. The revelation that his nature is Trinitarian brings us the knowledge that personal relationships are ultimate reality, and are blissful. The revelation of his character brings us the knowledge of how we may go about establishing our relationship with God and with one another more perfectly, by loving God with all our heart and loving our neighbour as ourselves, by giving ourselves in personal communication to one another, by

63 "No man is to be ordained without a charge, neither presbyter, nor deacon, nor anyone who is in the ecclesiastical order; but whoever is ordained must be appointed particularly to some charge in a church of a city, or in the country, or in a martyr or monastery. But as regards those who are ordained without any charge, the holy synod has determined, that such an ordination is to be held void, and cannot have any effect anywhere, to the reproach of the ordainer" (Council of Chalcedon, canon 6, 451).

absolute fairness and faithfulness in our dealings with each other, and by being mindful of the order and priority which God has created, so that our relationships may flower with the bliss that God intends for us in our friendship with him and with one another.

Matthias Media is an evangelical publishing ministry that seeks to persuade all Christians of the truth of God's purposes in Jesus Christ as revealed in the Bible, and equip them with high-quality resources, so that by the work of the Holy Spirit they will:

- abandon their lives to the honour and service of Christ in daily holiness and decision-making
- pray constantly in Christ's name for the fruitfulness and growth of his gospel
- speak the Bible's life-changing word whenever and however they can—in the home, in the world and in the fellowship of his people.

It was in 1988 that we first started pursuing this mission, and in God's kindness we now have more than 300 different ministry resources being used all over the world. These resources range from Bible studies and books through to training courses and audio sermons.

To find out more about our large range of very useful resources, and to access samples and free downloads, visit our website:

www.matthiasmedia.com

How to buy our resources

1. Direct from us over the internet:
   - in the US: www.matthiasmedia.com
   - in Australia and the rest of the world: www.matthiasmedia.com.au
2. Direct from us by phone:
   - in the US: 1 866 407 4530
   - in Australia: 1300 051 220
   - international: +61 2 9233 4627
3. Through a range of outlets in various parts of the world. Visit **www.matthiasmedia.com/contact** for details about recommended retailers in your part of the world, including www.thegoodbook.co.uk in the United Kingdom.
4. Trade enquiries can be addressed to:
   - in the US and Canada: sales@matthiasmedia.com
   - in Australia and the rest of the world: sales@matthiasmedia.com.au

Register at our website for our **free** regular email update to receive information about the latest new resources, **exclusive special offers**, and free articles to help you grow in your Christian life and ministry.

The How and Why of Love

by Michael Hill

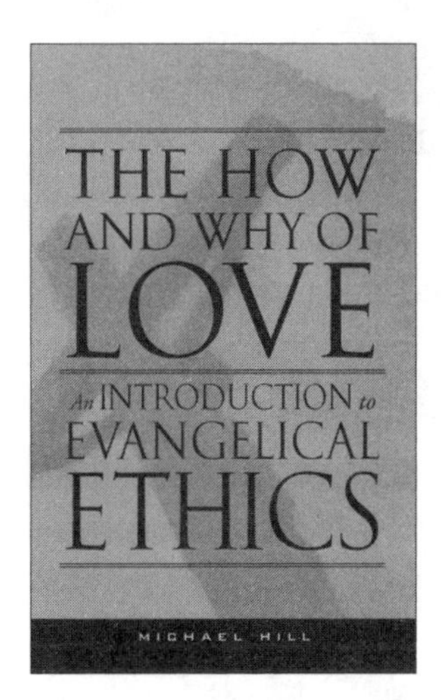

Is abortion ever right? Can divorced Christians remarry? What about euthanasia? In a whole range of issues, Christians search for the biblical answer. But ethics is about far more than controversial issues and hard cases. It's about how we apply the teaching of the Bible to our lives each day as we wait for Christ's return; it's about our actions and our motives; it's about our character.

In this vibrant, stimulating and much-needed book, Michael Hill introduces us to an evangelical approach to ethics. Starting from creation, and taking us through the whole of biblical theology, the author develops a simple and yet comprehensive model of gospel-based ethics. In so doing, he provides us not just with solutions to difficult cases, but with an ethical framework we can bring to every aspect of our lives.

Also available from Matthias Media

The Essence of the Reformation

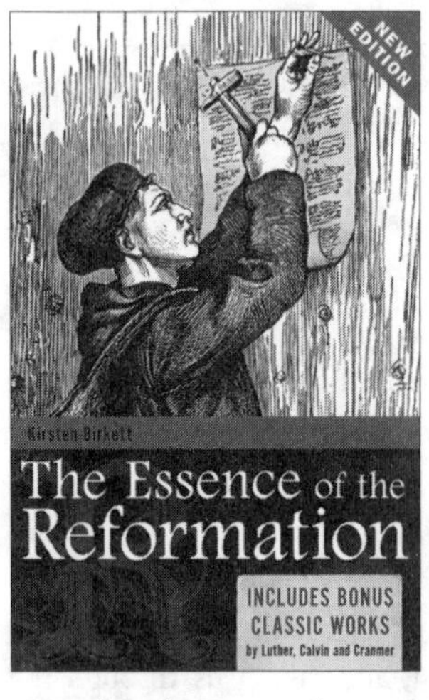

Corruption in the church. Political turmoil and intrigue. A clash of new ideas and ancient pagan religions. Courageous and extraordinary individuals. Doctrinal disputes that were matters of life and death.

These things and more make up what is called 'the Reformation', that tumultuous period of European history ranging from around 1517 to the turn of the century. The Reformation made our modern world what it is, and yet many people today have very little idea of even the basic events and people involved.

In this short introduction, Kirsten Birkett brings us the essence of the Reformation—the social and religious soil in which it grew, the events and people that shaped it, and the ideas and doctrines for which many of them died.

Also includes three classic works from the Reformation: Martin Luther on freedom, John Calvin on prayer and Thomas Cranmer on salvation.

I do not know any book that more succinctly gets across, in readable prose, what the Reformation was about. This new edition combines Birkett's superb text with some judiciously selected primary documents.
DA Carson

FOR MORE INFORMATION OR TO ORDER, CONTACT:

Matthias Media
Ph: 1300 051 220
Int: +61 2 9233 4627
Email: sales@matthiasmedia.com.au
www.matthiasmedia.com.au

Matthias Media (USA)
Ph: 1 866 407 4530
Int: +1 330 953 1702
Email: sales@matthiasmedia.com
www.matthiasmedia.com